Additional Praise for *Glamour Magic*

"With wit and good humor, Castellano offers up a series of 'experiments'—rituals and visualizations perfumed with hints of history, myth, pop culture and personal experience—that will lace your magic into a corset of enchantment that will steal your breath, but shape and sharpen your focus. Are you ready to unlock the power that lies within? You'll find the keys in *Glamour Magic*. Just. Say. Yes."

—Natalie Zaman, author of *Magical Destinations of the Northeast*

"An unapologetic Witch, Deborah takes you on an journey to unlock your personal power and embrace all that you are. The *Glamour Magic* exercises are powerful tools to awaken your inner Witch. This is a book to inspire and motivate you."

—Jacki Smith, founder of Coventry Creations and
author of *Coventry Magic with Candles, Oils, and Herbs*

"Deb recaptures the idea of the Witch as Enchantress and lays out the work, both magical and mundane, needed to fascinate and charm anyone—even yourself."

—Jason Miller, author of *Protection & Reversal Magick*

"Solid advice on self-improvement wrapped in the transgressive strength of Witchcraft. Real power comes from within, and this book shows you how."

—Lupa, author of *Nature Spirituality From the Ground Up*

GLAMOUR
MAGIC

Photo by Hellion Photography

About the Author

Deborah Castellano (Bridgewater, New Jersey) is a writer, crafter, and glamour girl who serves as a frequent contributor to occult/Pagan sources such as Witchvox, PaganSquare, and *Witches & Pagans*. Visit her online at www.DeborahMCastellano.com.

To Write to the Author

If you wish to contact the author or would like more information about this book, please write to the author in care of Llewellyn Worldwide, and we will forward your request. Both the author and the publisher appreciate hearing from you and learning of your enjoyment of this book and how it has helped you. Llewellyn Worldwide cannot guarantee that every letter written to the author can be answered, but all will be forwarded. Please write to:

Deborah Castellano
℅ Llewellyn Worldwide
2143 Wooddale Drive
Woodbury, MN 55125-2989

Please enclose a self-addressed stamped envelope for reply,
or $1.00 to cover costs. If outside the USA, enclose
an international postal reply coupon.

Many of Llewellyn's authors have websites with additional information and resources. For more information, please visit www.llewellyn.com.

GLAMOUR MAGIC

THE WITCHCRAFT REVOLUTION TO GET WHAT YOU WANT

DEBORAH CASTELLANO

Llewellyn Publications
Woodbury, Minnesota

First Edition
First Printing, 2017

Book design by Bob Gaul
Cover design by Ellen Lawson
Editing by Laura Graves

Llewellyn Publications is a registered trademark of Llewellyn Worldwide Ltd.

Library of Congress Cataloging-in-Publication Data
Names: Castellano, Deborah, author.
Title: Glamour magic: the witchcraft revolution to get what you want /
   Deborah Castellano.
Description: First edition. | Woodbury, Minnesota: Llewellyn Publications,
   [2017] | Includes bibliographical references and index.
Identifiers: LCCN 2017026783 (print) | LCCN 2017012906 (ebook) | ISBN
   9780738752679 (ebook) | ISBN 9780738750385 (alk. paper)
Subjects: LCSH: Witchcraft. | Magic. | Glamour.
Classification: LCC BF1566 (print) | LCC BF1566 .C324 2017 (ebook) | DDC
   133.4/3—dc23
LC record available at https://lccn.loc.gov/2017026783

Llewellyn Worldwide Ltd. does not participate in, endorse, or have any authority or responsibility concerning private business transactions between our authors and the public.

All mail addressed to the author is forwarded, but the publisher cannot, unless specifically instructed by the author, give out an address or phone number.

Any Internet references contained in this work are current at publication time, but the publisher cannot guarantee that a specific location will continue to be maintained. Please refer to the publisher's website for links to authors' websites and other sources.

Llewellyn Publications
A Division of Llewellyn Worldwide Ltd.
2143 Wooddale Drive
Woodbury, MN 55125-2989
www.llewellyn.com

Printed in the United States of America

CONTENTS

For Uncle Sock (Always)

All is
Fair in
Glamour
Warfare

Are you ready to revolutionize your magical practice by learning to use your glamour? Glamour is the perfect tool for a revolution because a revolution is started by a whisper, not a gunshot. Your glamour. Your whisper. Not into the deepest well in the forest, but into the right ear. You must tug on the heartstrings of modern-day queens and warlords who have power over you so that you can obtain whatever you desire most. This whisper could unlock windows, open doors, and slide through secret passages for your Great Work. You must be brave because you may only have one chance to ask for your most sacred wish from this powerful person. Your words will act as a straight shot of potent elixir that has been torn from your still-beating heart. It will hurt as it is ripped out of you. It will be terrifying once the whisper leaves your mouth. It risks everything. *You* risk everything.

Do you dare?

Your heart's desire always comes at a cost. If it were easily obtained, you would not want it so badly. There is always the dark of the dreamlike woods you must force yourself to walk. Here the wicked things hide and your great and small battles reside. Bits of you must be taken by your goddesses and spirits; friends will become enemies and then friends again; you'll see unexpected mercy shown from harsh rivals; hollow victories and cordial defeats; lost causes will be won; sure bets will be lost; high roads and low roads must be walked. You must be willing to have your face down in the mud with everything that ever mattered to you snatched up by the impassive Moirai and then equally ready to seize opportunity when they have inexplicably begun to favor you again. You must be cunning, you must be sly, you must be willing to employ tactics that aren't considered fair.

Like glamour.

What Is Glamour, Anyway?

The word *glamour* has two definitions:

1. What makes you exciting and interesting to others.

2. An illusionary spell.

The second definition is useless to us. It encourages dismissal from the actual community of Witches because it's easy to get swept up in the Hollywood special effects aspect of it. *Magic doesn't work like that*, our elders scold us. *And that's a wasteful use of it anyway, even if it could work like that.* It is quickly dismissed as a bad sleight-of-hand trick. You could change the color of your eyes a lot faster with contacts than concentrating large swaths of your magical practice dedicated to it. And so, glamour is dismissed as a not-terribly-realistic party trick instead of an earthshaking subtle magic that utilizes what makes you exciting and interesting to others.

It's no coincidence that glamour is also associated with female beauty, especially if this beauty dares to be tarted up by cosmetics or clothing. We have been taught that women "who try too hard" were never actually pretty, it was just their deceptive lipstick, their Spanx full of lies, their deceitfully glittering Manolo Blahniks. The lesson has been that if anyone dares to attempt to own their power, not with sheer dominance but by embracing all that is in them that is fascinating and charming to others—if they dared to try to make themselves into something that they wanted or actually reach for their heart's desire especially by using magic, their appearance, cunning, or bravery—they must be smacked down and shamed. Society relentlessly tells us that a real person of substance would never become involved in actually using glamour (definition one or two) of any kind to improve their lot in life. That sort of behavior is reserved for strippers, social climbers, those without means, drag kings and queens, people of dubious gender and sexual identity, drifters, grifters—and you. Yes, you.

Are You a Good Witch or a Bad Witch?

Witch. Occultist. Mage. Whatever word you have pressed into your own forehead and sealed in with blood, spit, or myrrh oil, we are Other. We have more in common with spies, assassins, pirates, and highwaymen than with the general modern populace. We may not live at the edge of the thick forest glen where we are given sacred offerings for our services anymore, but times change and so do we. Glamour isn't a magic of landscapes that never really existed—it's everything interesting and exciting about you that you already have residing inside you. If it's already there, lying dormant and sleeping in the bottom of your brainpan, in the slope of your stomach, in the crook of your nethers, what can't you accomplish once you know how to use it? We are used to being denied as Other. We have become accustomed to accepting less and apologizing for everything we are that is not easily accepted (yes, even now). We apologetically ask our goddesses, spirits, and ancestors for only what we feel like we actually deserve, and then just a little less to be sure. We must never be seen by anyone *ever* as someone who overreached, as someone who grasped, as someone who is acquisitive. Not by our families, not by our friends, not by our communities, not even by the universe herself.

Think of faery tales, think of reality television shows, think of operas. Who's the cautionary tale? It's the Bad Girl. The one who took more than she should have, the one who asked for retribution, the one who forgot her place, the one who didn't need to be liked by others if she could further her cause. She is the one who must be destroyed, she is the one who must cry at the bottom of a well for her misdeeds, she is the one who must be thrown down at all costs. No matter what your gender, you may identify with the Bad Girl archetype if you have ever been made to feel "less than," if you have ever been scapegoated or berated simply for standing up for yourself when it wasn't convenient for others, if you've ever solved a problem with a strategy others wouldn't dare.

Nice Girls are the ones who are rewarded. They must be patient, obedient, and kind, not for the sake of any of these virtues themselves, but so they will be rescued and rewarded. So we force ourselves to be Nice Girls, because we shiver at the consequences we've seen through cultural narratives and in the satisfaction we've seen others take when a real-life Bad Girl is dethroned. No matter how much this role chafes us, we will grit our teeth because this is how our narrative will move forward. It is the only way to ask for something—politely—and just a little bit less than we want. It's the only way to receive anything for ourselves without shuddering about our enemies. If we are righteous, we will be worthy. We wait, we do what we are supposed to do, and we keep hoping until we are bitter that our virtue was not rewarded nor was it enough of a reward in and of itself. Whatever your gender identity, you may find yourself relating to being a Good Girl if you would rather go along to get along even if it puts your personal ambition at stake, if you are courteous even when the time for courtesy has long since passed, or if you follow an intricate set of rules to be well-liked by others. We all have something in common here as Nice Girls: being nice didn't make our most illicit wishes manifest.

What if it were possible to be Bad while still being Good?

You can be both of those things. You can be Bad enough to work to get your aspiration fulfilled using mundane work, glamour, and magic while still being Good enough to have a personal code of ethics that keeps your head held up high.

It starts right here, right now with your Great Work.

Your Great Work Is Fueled by Your Desire

In alchemy, your Great Work would refer to your creation of a Philosopher's Stone, which would go through four stages of development and be used to make you a more powerful alchemist and possibly immortal. Colors, birds, and other symbols would assist you through the Work, but your Philosopher's Stone would be created by you for your personal enlightenment. Your power, the materials you have selected, your interpretation of the texts, and your ambitions for yourself would greatly affect the Stone's creation.

When I refer to your Great Work, I am referring to your innermost transmutation, which begins when you are able to pinpoint what you want. Yes. *Want*—the real heart of the dark in your everyday life faery story. Witchcraft is meant to be used for those who want something as much as a faery tale's heroine or villain. If you didn't have a blaze of unfulfilled need within you, why would you go on a journey that will have unknown and terrifying consequences? You won't be able to map out every step of this path, you won't know what will be asked of you to feed that fire, and you don't know if you will succeed. What will it bring into your life? What will it take away? No sensible person would travel down murky, unknown corridors unless...they wanted something fiercely in the dark of their heart. Before we make our first step on this journey, however, we require...

A Syllabus for Our Ritual Esoteric Experiments

A ritual can be as simple or as elaborate as you make it. You are captain of your own ship. You can decide for yourself what works best for yourself in the Esoteric Experiments you'll find throughout this book. That being said, I encourage you to step outside of your most comfortable Witchcraft habits and investigate practicing in different ways. Comfort often does not guarantee success. For example, I personally have a reality television habit I have recently (mostly) broken. It's comfortable and makes me feel invested but prevents me from using my time to practice Witchcraft, read, write, practice yoga, actively engage with others, or watch plot-driven television. So I must (mostly, at least) break this deliciously comfortable habit if I want to see real change in other aspects of my life.

If you generally cast a circle, don't. Use another method of protection. If you usually refrain from asking your goddesses and spirits for small favors, ask and see what happens. If you are usually carefully choreographed, see how your Work works when you are more improvisational. Keep notes as to what you've done that is different than what you usually do and what results you see from your altered Work. It's very difficult to change habits that bring us comfort, but Witchcraft was never designed to make us safe or comfortable. Witchcraft was created to shake up the world both externally and internally. It's a primal scream that demands to be heard.

The rites (Esoteric Experiments) in this book are meant to be accomplished in the order they are presented. Each experiment's design is meant to spark your own creativity; they are not meant to be used as an exact format but as a compass rose to point you in the correct direction in finding the intended objective. However you choose to find that objective is up to you, the important aspect is finding it. You can disregard all of my suggestions in the Esoteric Experiments or follow them as closely as you wish, it's up to you.

If you choose to go out of order or choose to skip any, there will not be generational curses laid on your head, spirits will not hunt you in your sleep, nor any of those exciting things. That said, if you would like to actually manifest your glamour and leverage it into accomplishing your Great Work, it would behoove you to carefully and thoughtfully do each ritual in the order it's presented.

Much like your DNA, fingerprints, and personality, no one's Great Works are going to be exactly alike. Your Great Work needs to be something that takes effort for you to accomplish, it should be something that is deeply meaningful to you, and it should be something that needs both practical work and magical work to complete. Potential Great Works can be anything from *Having a regular spiritual practice* to *Finding a mate to marry* to *Discovering my career path* to *Accomplishing a specific creative endeavor* to *Buying a house so I can put down roots*. This first Esoteric Experiment will help you discover what your Great Work is, and throughout the book you will be given opportunities to use your glamour magic to give you more opportunities to obtain your Great Work.

***

Esoteric Experiment No. 1

Objective: Discover your first Great Work.

Pack your bag with things you may need and can carry. A leather journal gifted to you that you've never used and a good pen. A curated playlist for your phone. A vintage blanket. A travel carafe filled with kava tea. A scone you baked with carefully chosen herbs. Battered tarot cards. Well-worn mala beads. A compass that belonged to your grandmother. Drawing pencils and heavy paper. A scent that evokes a particular memory. Sturdy boots. A well-worn sweater. A small packet of salt. A second small packet of unadulterated tobacco. A protective amulet. Pomegranate seeds. A lipstick as red as the rose. A compact mirror etched with clandestine sigils. A sacred text. An enchanted salve.

Go into the woods. No, not there. Not your forest with the tree that cradles you within its limbs and the blackbirds that sing back to you. It must be an unfamiliar grove that has no memory of you. Follow the trails laid out for you by helpful strangers until you are deeply enmeshed in this foreign copse. Walk until you find trees that croon to you, walk until you find a place that feels a part of your kismet. Step off the trail while being mindful of how to get back to it. Amble until you find a place that is clandestine. Place your blanket down. First, offer your tobacco to the forest. Say words that are simple and natural to you. Lay your offering down at the base of a tree. Demarcate your working space and create a protection for yourself by arranging a ring of salt around your blanket. Turn a piece of your clothing inside out. Arrange the objects from your carrier on your blanket until you are satisfied. Set your intention. Word your desire to find your Great Work carefully and concisely. Employ your chosen objects to assist you. Freewrite. Draw. Alter your headspace. Trance out to your playlist. Draw cards until a path is clear. Eat pomegranate seeds until your spirits manifest. Mantra: Sooo *(inhale)* Hummm *(exhale). I am that. Look for signs and omens in the birds, the trees, the squirrels, the deer. Stay until you have a concise, one-sentence Great Work. Remain there, past the boredom, past the frustration, past the anger, past the existential angst, past the chattering in your brain. Persist until you have your answer. This is your quest. This is the beginning of your journey.*

Write down your heart's desire in one sentence. The thrill of fear that runs through you after writing it down so boldly is real. But if you are careful, if you are cunning, if you use the sorcery that pulses within you, you may just live to tell the tale. If it doesn't burn you alive like a powdery white moth first, of course. Don't say I didn't warn you.

Glamour isn't just a flame, it's a bonfire.

Now That You Know What You Want, How Will You Get It?

Now that you've discovered your Great Work, do you find yourself surprised by what you found it to be? Is it something you always knew you had burning inside you? Take a breath and take a little time to start to plan the mundane work needed to accomplish it. Use whatever method works for you: sketching, writing, using an organizer, collecting photos, or whatever is organic to your process. Starting to brainstorm about how to practically accomplish your Great Work will put you in the right mindset to do the glamour magic to attain it.

Once you've brainstormed a bit, here are some practical tools to break down your Great Work:

1. Start telling people about your Great Work. Nothing motivates someone like the shame of being too lazy to accomplish what you set out to achieve. Telling other people also gives you the advantage of having cheerleaders to encourage you when you fail and give you praise when you succeed.

2. Break it down. Let's say you want to start your own business. That's a long process, as I know from experience. It's too big in that form; you will get distracted by Facebook. What's a good starting point for that Great Work? Looking into what kind of business, then looking into what you need to succeed in that kind of business. Start it as side-hustle with social media and a website, and *then* see if it's everything you wanted it to be. Perform glamour magic to bring in the right influences. Consider how you would want to present yourself in your business. Make a mission statement. Figure out what you would need accomplish with this business for you to quit your day job, save some more money as a cushion, and so on and so on. You need to break it down into reasonable steps while still allowing for failure and unforeseen circumstances, both positive and negative.

3. Be disciplined, be committed. If you have a deadline for aspects of your Great Work, you need to hit them. Even without deadlines, the best way to accomplish your Great Work is through…well, work. Makes sense, no? You need to be hustling and grinding both in your glamour and practical work. If you aren't constantly working on your Great Work, it won't be accomplished. It will just be

another lost dream. You may be wondering, *what does constant work mean?* If someone asked you what you've done recently to move forward with your Great Work, do you immediately have an answer? Are you sick of your Great Work? Have you started to secretly hate it? If you said *yes* to all of those questions, then you're in the right place.

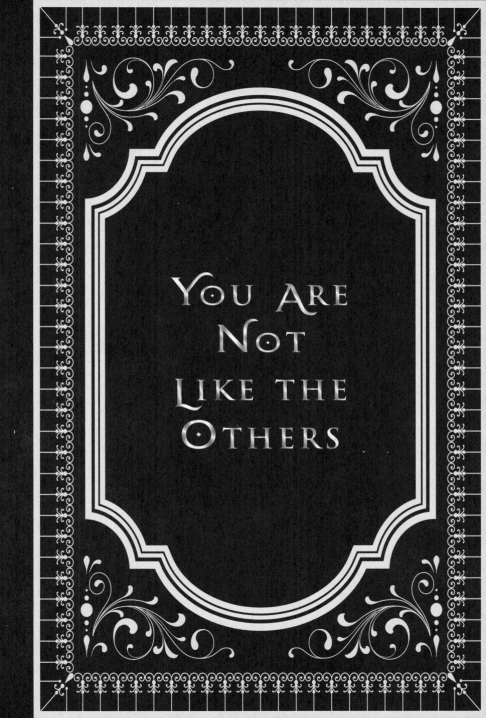

YOU ARE
NOT
LIKE THE
OTHERS

As Witches, we have learned to defang ourselves in exchange for a place for ourselves in small towns, cities, and suburbs. It would be an actual falsehood to deny that it's beneficial for us to have at least a thin veneer of respectability.

So, we give fresh water infused with mint and homemade meringue cookies with smiles to our suburban neighbors at Pagan Prides. We head up committees on the PTA. We walk our dogs and adopt cats at our local shelters. We serve in the military. We fast our hands together in marriage, we give birth to tiny babies with names full of unfulfilled promise. We live in condos and cottages, we work in the media, we work in accounting, we work in hospitals, we honor our (recent) ancestral familial heritage at Christmas, at Rosh Hashanah, at Ramadan, at family reunions. We are everywhere. We want everyone to sleep well at night with the knowledge that we're just like everyone else. There's nothing to fear, we offer chanting for peace and volunteer at our local food co-operatives.

So much the better to mask what we do alone and together in the dark of the moon.

Make no mistake about it, we are Other. Whenever you are removed from the dominant narrative in your culture, you become Other. If you are a woman in a traditionally masculine role, you are Other. If you are a man in a traditionally feminine role, you are Other. If you don't identify as a gender at all—let's stop right there, you are Other.

Tolerance Is Not the Same as Acceptance

But! But! So many pop culture Witches! I wear my preferred Witchcraft symbol in a noticeable place and no one bothers me! We, like, worked totally hard for chaplains in the US military to acknowledge us and when they bury us for dying for this country, we now have four whole symbols to choose from!

Right. Except almost every pop culture Witch I can think of off-hand has to be punished in their narrative. In *Buffy the Vampire Slayer,* Willow is considered a Witch with an addiction to magic and is punished for it when her girlfriend, Tara (also a Witch) is murdered. In *Wicked,* Elphie is dead in the end of the book version (though may someday come back to life) and has to leave Oz forever. In the musical version, she is unable to tell Glinda that she survived. Glinda is trapped in Oz with all of her loved ones gone and forced into a role that she may no longer want. So you're punished if you're an outcast and punished if you play the game too, making Oz a very enticing locale for Witches.

In *Frozen,* Elsa is not permitted a love interest, though Hans could have very easily been written as non-villainous and a love interest for Elsa or Anna, leaving Kristoff for the remaining "unmatched" sister (It is still Disney after all). In *Practical Magic,* the aunts are marginalized in their community for practicing the Craft. Prue Halliwell in *Charmed* is double punished—when she becomes a "super Witch," she's killed by a demon. It's a double punishment because Shannon Doherty couldn't get along with the publicly better-liked Alyssa Milano, which is (allegedly) the reason she got kicked off the show, never to be seen again. And the kill list for *American Horror Story: Coven*? Too long to even get into.

We can be more public with our Craft, but how often do you actually meaningfully talk about it with authority figures in your life? No one would ever tell you that you were fired or excluded due to your beliefs, but they could certainly find other reasons to give for letting you go or not including you. Does that silence you?

As a Witch who is part of the Other by virtue of refusing to submit to the monolithic religions in power in a first-world country, you are expected to behave in a certain way to fit into society. You are expected to be a shining example of morality; you are expected to keep altars in your home that will not make others uncomfortable, you are to have a career where you help others, you are to only use your power for the good of yourself and others, you are expected to behave within your community's code of social mores. You are expected to work harder to prove yourself to those in power, which typically means showing that you are just like them except for this one teensy thing (Witchcraft. But also: sexual orientation, gender identity, dis/ability, ethnicity, social class. The more Other you have in you, the less palatable you are to those in power as you create more disruption to the ruling order). Then, if you are deemed good enough by those who hold power over you by being a shining example despite your Otherness, you may be given some crumbs from their table and be allowed some nominal power.

That is the route of the Good Girl. If you are a Good Girl, the only kind of Other you can be is one who allows herself to be commodified by her "betters" and trotted out as a show pony who can perform on command and make everyone else feel educated and tolerant. You will read tarot on command, you will heal on command, and you will produce an open circle that can be attended by all on command. When your oppressors show you where your place is supposed to be, you accept it graciously and gratefully. If you have the option to tone down your practice to make others more comfortable, you are to always choose that option. You are a Very Special episode of *Degrassi* or *Skins* where it is your goddess-given *duty* to educate, advocate, and never ever make a mistake that cannot be immediately corrected with your tears washing your oppressors' feet.

Or you could be a Bad Girl. Bad Girls are there to function as fetishes in the Witchcraft community. What freaky things can you do in bed for me under the watchful eyes of your goddesses (or better, demons!) in your bedroom? What hexes will you lay down for me if I pay you enough or give you what you want? What will you wear to the school board meeting so I can disapprovingly cluck my tongue? You are there to be a cautionary tale of what happens when you are subjected to a twenty-mile radius of fear, suspicion, and jealousy. You are the sand in their eye, the rock in their shoe, the pea under their mountain of Good Girl mattresses. You need to be held down and thrown down whenever possible because you disrupt your local cultural narrative. You are the enemy. The Witch who must be stopped from accomplishing anything. You must be silenced as soon as possible. You must be kept from having lovers, family, friends, along with any commonly accepted measure of success. Any mistake you make will be told over and over again in languorous detail to remind your Good Girl sisters what happens when a bitch forgets her place.

Or, you could recognize that every small decision you make has the possibility to subtly claim power over someone else, and you can work to use these small decisions that you make to reclaim your agency. If you make enough of these small decisions, you may just cause a micro-rebellion for yourself. All through your day you are making tiny decisions to have power over someone or something else. The food you eat that comes from animals and plants that had to be sacrificed to sustain you, the text messages you dodge because you don't want to deal with the proffered drama, when you refuse to back down from a decision even though it makes others' lives more difficult, sending your child to bed an hour early because they cannot tell time yet and you have had enough for one day— these are all "power over" decisions. Small "power over" decisions, but "power over" decisions nonetheless.

Witchcraft is a tool of the oppressed to find an advantage in a world that has given us significantly less advantage than others. It's why the wealthy traditionally (and currently) outsource their deeds to a Witch versus becoming a Witch themselves. They want to know that it's being taken care of, they don't want to dirty their hands in it.

This Is Your Secret Power—Use It

Think about it this way: old, straight, privileged, white dudebros have never been particularly concerned about how money and power will alter their personalities. There is no hand-wringing about how having privilege will change their relationships with others because it's not a concern. They accept money, prestige, and power as what the world owes them and go about their business running the world. Perhaps it's time that we stopped worrying about what isn't our place and obsessing over how our actions could possibly inconvenience others and fight for ourselves and our Great Works.

You might be concerned that all of this potential power will change who you are internally in unexpected ways, which is a valid concern. If done correctly, you will. Your moral compass may shift, you could make regrettable mistakes along the way, you could learn difficult things about yourself. Glamour is guerilla warfare, which is why it is not to be taken lightly. Especially since it's not a fight you will always win. How badly do you want your heart's deepest desire?

If you are still unsure that Witchcraft qualifies as Otherness, I invite you to partake in this optional social experiment.

(Optional) Social Experiment No. 1

Objective: Learn a loved one's
true feelings about Witchcraft.

Step One: *Among your non-magical circle of family, friends, and acquaintances who know you are a Witch, wait for one of them to have a semi-serious problem with someone else. Perhaps this antagonist is causing problems for your loved one in the workplace, perhaps your loved one has a troublesome ex-lover, perhaps there are landlord issues. Listen to the problem.*

Step Two: *Ask your loved one if she would like you to magically work on the antagonist causing her problems. Do* *not give any standard Craft modifiers to this statement. Standard Craft modifiers include, "Positive energy only!" "I only work with white magic!" "I would never work on another person without her permission!" Even if those statements are true of your personal practice, do not say them. If asked if you plan on doing any black magic on the antagonist, be noncommittal about it. Shrug, say you're not sure yet.*

Step Three: *Watch your loved one closely for a reaction. In the majority of cases, you will see something like fear and/ or repulsion on his face along with a hasty, "No thank you!" regardless of your loved one's personal beliefs or moral code. The minority will want you to work on their antagonist, in which case offer to help in whatever way you would generally magically assist someone according to your own code of ethics. Most people don't want to be Macbeth to your Lady Macbeth, even if their waking-self claims not to believe in Witchcraft.*

I invite you to step into that Otherness and to make it a cornerstone of your Craft. There is strength in embodying the unknown, the discarded, the feared. Some of you may be fretting that this may lead to "power over" versus "power with." If you are using it correctly, it should lead to exactly that. Make the odds be ever in your favor. Starting now.

It's not enough in your Great Work for you to blend in with the general masses. If that was enough it would be called a mediocre work. Your Otherness gives you power, your Otherness enhances your glamour, your Otherness can potentially give your Great Work opportunities because you are different.

Esoteric Experiment No. 2

Objective: Step into your Otherness.

Wear clothing that feels most like an expression of you. Choose music that feels most expressive of you. Gather tiny representations of your Otherness that are meaningful to you. Charms, herbs, bones, stones, pictures, whatever is special to you. Use a small scrap of cloth from a piece of your clothing that you cannot wear anymore and is too damaged to donate. Wrap your objects in this piece of cloth. Use yarn to wrap your packet closed. Over your packet, breathe your intention for stepping into your Otherness. Breathe your intention for your Otherness to help you achieve your Great Work. Breathe your intention for your Otherness to be part of your glamour. Keep your packet in your pocket, your bra, or purse until you feel firmly entrenched in your Otherness. Then, keep it on your altar or bedside table.

Your Actions Have Consequences

Now that we've decided that we are serious about this adventure, let's discuss what actually needs to be done here. On one hand, it is *easier* (morality aside) to go into the woods, find the maiden who is prettier than you, and cut out her heart yourself thus making you the prettiest pretty forever and ever, amen. It would be less of a challenge if you simply needed to commit some forbidden, bloody act and then be granted your wish. That's the seductive part of the faery tale, the sluagh in the woods who promises you a life away from your despised parents in Faeryland if you murder them first.

Perhaps, for some of us, it *is* that simple. Dark deeds, pacts with the right demons, and then it's a smooth path to your longing that doesn't require you to change, be inconvenienced, or work harder than you wanted to; everything is just as you imagined. I can't say that I know anyone (or even the urban legend "friend of a friend") who has had that kind of luck or grace regarding the occult, so I feel safe in saying I sincerely doubt that will be the case for you.

Your journey to achieving your purpose won't look the way you imagined it to be, so your success (should you be so un/lucky) won't look the way you envisioned it either. You will have long, dark moments where it feels like you are lost in your internal Schwarzwald Forest, no better than Hansel or Gretel. People who genuinely care for you will openly doubt you... and you will doubt yourself. You will be rejected in places that wound you. All of your flaws, all of your faults, all of your tender points will be spewed up for you like a fountain of black tar. You will wonder if all of your suffering, all of your pain, all of your anxiety will make it worth it to achieve your coveted longing.

Maybe. Maybe it will be.

But maybe it won't be.

What you *think* you want and what you actually want aren't always the same thing; sometimes it is quite the bitter discovery to learn the difference.

None of this matters. I can tell you that the oven is hot and will burn you, that boy will only break your heart, and eating belladonna will kill you. But if you are bound to step onto a path, nothing will stop you. It certainly never stopped me.

However, if you would like to be successful in achieving your wish however advised or ill-advised it may be, you must look at it holistically. Do the work. All of it. Do the tedious tasks that don't require candlelight. Do the work that requires you to enlist others to aid you, letting your glamour engulf them into your cause. Do the Witchcraft that leads you into a deeper understanding of your desire and casts the odds in your favor. Do the work you are avoiding. Do the work that makes you uncomfortable. Do the work even when your passion has died and you would rather watch YouTube videos instead.

That said, however badly you want your Great Work, you also need to be able to sleep at night. Glamour, just like any other magic, has a price.

Magically speaking, it will be difficult to see if your magical work is having an effect on your karma because karma is actually a super complicated process that is based off of good deeds and bad deeds over lifetimes and weighed out by various bureaucratic spirits and goddesses who are tasked with the tedious job of keeping track of when you are naughty and when you are nice. The law of three is a very nice story that keeps our neighbors easy around us. After all, if we only practice white magic and we are all only Good Witches, there is nothing to fear if they transgress against us. Without an easy-to-follow rhetoric that promises to keep us in line, what couldn't we do? Getting tied up into Good Girl morality tales of being rewarded due to virtue and Bad Girl morality tales of being punished due to disregarding social mores isn't going to help you here.

What *will* help you is to determine what behavior and magic you think is acceptable to your own moral compass and what behavior and magic you think is unacceptable to your moral compass. Do you feel sick to your stomach at the idea of double-crossing a coworker? Does the idea of hexing your enemies make you feel uneasy and upset? Would seducing your sister's husband make you feel eaten alive with guilt? Here's an idea: Maybe don't do those things.

Perhaps, you see yourself as someone who is more morally flexible. Perhaps manipulating a situation in the workplace where you look great and a coworker you can't stand gets fired doesn't bother you. You may believe that a Witch needs to be able to hex as well as heal. Maybe you want to show your sister who's in control by sleeping with her husband. Maybe none of this bothers you.

I'm not here to shake my finger disapprovingly at morally questionable acts or bully you into committing yourself to acts that are outside your moral code. I *am* here to tell you that you have to be able to live with yourself every day, no matter what. I can't tell you where those lines should be. I can tell you that it's entirely likely that you will make some mistakes and inadvertently step outside your moral boundaries while practicing glamour magic. I can also tell you that if you ever leave your house and engage with other people on any kind of level, you are equally likely to accidently make moral mistakes because that's life as a human.

Where does that leave you? It leaves you as a Witch. A Witch is someone who is not constrained by always doing the societally accepted "right thing" to appease others and who may be inclined to actively work against those who would harm her or prevent him from achieving his goals. A Witch is *also* someone who may not want to ever actively work against someone and may find it morally repugnant to engage in certain acts both mundanely and magically. Which Witch you are is up to you and only you. You may start out as one kind and then find yourself as the other; you may find yourself in some kind of morally gray middle ground. But it is vital that a Witch has a strong grasp on their own personal moral compass and works to live within their own moral code of ethics.

It can be a heady time when you are coming in to your glamour, and it's understandable that you may find yourself either desiring to or actually wielding it rather injudiciously. However, finding a situation understandable is not the same as finding it excusable. *Ignorantia juris non excusat.* You need to be able to think critically about your magic, your spirits and goddesses, the people you interact with, and your Great Work. This also includes learning to predict possible consequences of your actions and taking responsibility for them. Sometimes seeing harm come to another can be an action for which you are willing to take responsibility. Sometimes it is not. Only you and your moral compass know what is acceptable collateral damage for you to inflict upon the world at large.

Let's say you do something that another party finds morally questionable but you don't find it to have been a morally questionable action. You need to be able to stand in your action and accept that the other party may not agree that it was the right thing to do. It's not your place to convince the other party that you somehow had the moral high ground because it's likely you didn't. You felt the ends justified the means. And maybe they did. But that doesn't suddenly excuse you from consequences from that action. Other parties may disassociate themselves from you due to that action, it may be poorly received in your local community or workplace, it may have unforeseen consequences years down the line that you did not anticipate. You need to decide if these potential repercussions are an outcome you can live with. If they are, *bonne chance*. If they're not, here's that crazy idea again: don't do it.

Most importantly, no matter if your intention was pure and good and then somehow went off the rails, was slightly bad then got out of hand, or was a bad action you had planned but did not like the result of, you need to take responsibility for your actions when you transgress. Avoid "butbutbut magic—" as in, "But, but, but I didn't mean to!" No one else cares about that when you hurt them. Intention may help the other party understand why you did what you did, but that's not an apology. Defensiveness is not an apology. Casting blame on others is not an apology. An apology is "I'm sorry for doing x to you. How can I fix our relationship?"

Glamour is not for the faint of heart. You need to be able to own every action you commit and when you misstep, you need to be able to apologize for it and offer help. If you want to win your battles great and small, that will require other people. What you do to/with other people is up to you and only you know what is morally right and wrong for you. This is why you need to do a moral compass check before going any further.

Esoteric Experiment No. 3

Objective: Define your own moral code of ethics.

Find a place that is suitable for meditation: a shed in your backyard, your workroom, or an overnight camping trip in a secluded area. Twilight is the suggested time frame for this rite.

Select an activity that is physically vigorous for you: moon salutations, ecstatic dance, a long walk, lovemaking.

Encircle yourself with protective herbs. Cedar tips. Vervain. Acorns. Heather. If you feel you can safely surround yourself with a circle of glass-encased candles, do so. If you have doubts about setting your home, your yard, or a forest on fire, use a string of battery-operated LED faery lights to create an inner circle surrounding you. Burn a stick of palo santo wood in a heat-safe container. Wear something that flows—a tulle skirt, linen pants, a long cotton dress. Lie down in savasana (corpse) pose: palms facing upward, lying on your back, legs spread slightly apart. Take in tiny sips of air three beats apart. When you can no longer take in sips of air, exhale in a long breath. Do this until you feel centered.

Travel inward to places that are sacred to you. Consider possible actions and consequences. What do you find morally repugnant? What actions could you do in this life that are unforgiveable to your conscience? What would you find repulsive for someone else to do to you? Does that affect your decision on whether or not to do that to others? Are you willing to work on others for your own goals? What are your boundaries with that? Are there actions you could commit that your goddesses and spirits would find abhorrent? What would you do if you were caught in frowned upon actions? What would you do if someone started working on you due to your actions? Can you get out of a mess? When you feel you have put together a cognizant outline for your moral quandaries, you are now ready to move forward into the next stage of glamour: involving others.

Your Darkness and Your Light: Perfect Together

There is glamour in the darkness, in the evil queen, the Witch in the woods. There's something exciting about feathers, bone, and blood draped over wild hair, a dark cloak, and the cottage that could save you or suck the marrow from your bones. The stranger offering the maiden everything she ever wanted … with one small catch. Equally exciting is the dashing paladin, the Good Witch, the beloved queen. The beauty of the glittering armor, the jeweled crown, the drying herbs that smell of life and love. All of those things live inside you—the Bad Girl Turned Good, the Good Girl Gone Bad, the Patient Princess, the Dark Queen—but we tend to want to favor one over the other. Why? There is deep power in the intimate knowledge of the aspects of self that most shy away from, especially the parts of yourself that are Other and that you try to gentrify for the comfort of those around you.

When you know the great and terrible things that you are truly capable of, when you know what lives inside of you, that is when you truly own the space you stand in. Think of the savage beauty that comes from that knowledge, the wild constellation of glamour that will gleam out of every molecule of your skin. If you can harness all that is cruel and ferocious about yourself, all that is prodigious and beautiful, wouldn't the Moirai notice?

Esoteric Experiment No. 4

Objective: Learn truths you have hidden from yourself about yourself. Decipher how to use these truths to move you closer to achieving your Great Work and as part of your glamoury.

This rite is best performed during a waning moon in the evening. Use a windowless room with a door that can be shut, such as your bedroom closet. Choose a time and day when you will not be disturbed. Bathe yourself in the smoke of purifying herbs. Sage. Lavender. Rosemary. Dress simply in dark colors; leave your hair and face unadorned. Arrange your space in such a way as it is comfortable to you to sit for a potentially long period of time. Once arranged, ponder which of your ritual tools will assist you best in the dark. A black glass chalice filled with sacred water. A dark mirror. Prayer beads. A spirit dolly. Bones to throw. Softly played trance music. The sound of running water. Arrange your tools. Hang a protective amulet over the door inside your room. A hamsa, a Brigit's cross, a horseshoe. Darken the room and use your method of divination that you have chosen to begin your journey about your hidden truths. Stay in the space until you have found what you had concealed from yourself about your darkest and lightest pieces and consider how to use them both in achieving your Great Work and as fragments of your glamour, that which makes you most fascinating and exciting to others.

Your glamour won't look like anyone else's; it shouldn't. You aren't attempting to mimic an actress you aspire to be like; you are working toward being your best self. Your best self is just that—you at your best. It is you at your most clever, your most beautiful, your wittiest, your most cunning, your most compassionate, your most kind. You at peace with your darkness, your anger, your sadness, your grief, your insecurities.

All of these aspects will open doors in the universe to your Great Work. Stay with me. Glamour is despised and spat upon because it's an artificial construct. *We want what's most real!* No, you don't. You think you do; we all do. We think that's what love, beauty, and success are, effortless. If you look like you put a lot of effort into something, then somehow, inexplicably it becomes of less worth to others.

Let's be clear: This is a completely ridiculous notion. Anything worth doing is a lot of work. Glamour is such a fantastic form of Witchcraft because it's completely self-created. It's not about presenting a false front; it's about manipulating actual personality aspects that are within you and external constructs that others find interesting and attractive. If you don't care about long lashes, that's not going to be a cornerstone to your external glamour. If you think long lashes are glamorous but yours are short, you may find the perfect mascara or learn to put on false eyelashes because it's meaningful to you. If you don't have eyelashes and wanted to wear false eyelashes, that's your right and privilege, too. You didn't suddenly become a false version of yourself because you now have eyelashes/longer eyelashes when you previously didn't. Your new false eyelashes may give you a boost to be flirtier or bolder, but they're not going to make you knock over a bank if you weren't previously planning on doing so.

Reflect about what you learned about yourself in the fourth Esoteric Experiment. What did you decide were the best and worst parts of yourself? How can you work with these aspects to bend and shape how you present them to others? It's important to note that your glamour won't look like anyone else's, nor will you (or should you) become someone you aren't. You want to draw opportunities, influences, and people to you, not a false projection. In terms of Witchcraft, if you are presenting a completely false front, the energy you draw to it won't "stick" as well, because there's nothing really there to stick to.

Choose an aspect that is part of the light side of your glamour: your kindness, your charisma, your humor, your compassion, your adorableness, your intellect, your bravery, your resolution. Consider how to take a generically "good" trait and make it into something glamorous. Reflect on these two examples:

1. People think I'm smart.

2. People think I'm smart because I'm very knowledgeable about Hermeticism and I can talk about it in a way that's relatable and interesting even if the other person is new to it, both in person and on my blog.

The first one is good, but it's very general and it's hard to do much with. The second one is much more specific. You want to stand out in the minds of others (also including goddesses, spirits, and the universe) because that's how you make forward progress. Consider how to do that about this trait and find small ways in your daily life to "read" as specific in that trait and not generally in that aspect. Find a mantra for it, keep it simple. *My bravery is glamorous to myself and others.* Start building energy up inside you as you concentrate on how you see this aspect. Imagine this aspect's energy coming up from the ground, over your legs, over your back, and then over your head, over your throat, over your chest, over your stomach, over your sex, over your legs, and then cycle it back up, seven times. On the eighth time, when you draw it up, see yourself completely surrounded by this aspect. However you see this aspect, amplify it until it's an ocean within you of how you see this aspect. Focus on how this aspect will help you achieve your Great Work and what your Great Work will bring you until you feel encircled by this aspect of your glamour. Keep notes in your journal about how this affects your daily life. Keep working with this aspect until you notice change. Once you notice change in how you see yourself and how others treat you about this aspect, you can move on to a darker aspect.

Find the glamour in your darker aspects. Shyness can be glamorous. Sullenness can be glamorous. Ineptness can be glamorous. Hesitation can be glamorous. Angst can be glamorous. Melancholy can be glamorous. It's all in how you present it. On an energetic level, it's about how you project it. Which sounds enticing:

1. I haven't showered in a week, my clothes are stained because I can't bring myself to care, and I'm eating handfuls of cereal out of a box because I am too demotivated to do otherwise.

2. I have an air of sorrow about me, I wear a simple dress because I am too gloomy to be too concerned about fashion, and I make a humble meal of chicken and greens?

Both are essentially the same thing; you're depressed, you're miserable, and you are probably not doing as much as you feel you could. Both require approximately the same amount of effort, but one sounds sad, slumpy, and frumpy, and the other sounds more like a Brontë novel. How you see yourself affects how others (including goddesses and the universe) see you.

Think about how to shape your intent with this dark aspect of your glamour and put it out into the universe. How do you see this aspect? Are words attached to it? Feelings? Colors? Images? Sounds? Music? Scents? Really fully develop it internally. Your glamour is a part of you, so you get to decide how to mold it. How can you take this difficult aspect and make it attractive to yourself and others? How will you change some small daily habits to take it from tolerable to glamourous, both to yourself and others?

Do the energetic exercise described with the light trait now with the dark trait. Choose a simple mantra, *My gloom is glamorous to myself and others.* Continue to journal until you see change as we discussed and then continue to alternate between light traits and dark traits until you feel you have a good handle on how your glamour works as a cohesive aspect of your magic. You will know it's working when it feels more like a recipe you know by heart and don't have to think about to create it versus trying to cook a recipe for the first time (So many steps! So many small adjustments to make!).

Once you get a handle on these aspects, you'll be able to delve more deeply into your glamour toolbox, making you a formidable force for your autocrats: beauty, charm, discipline, conviction, and organization.

Glamour, Unwound

Beauty isn't what the oppressor-run media tells you is beautiful, but what people actually find beautiful in their day-to-day lives. Others will naturally want to help those they find attractive. Think about how you feel about baby animals. You naturally want to help them because they are so tiny and adorable. It's the same for many people with human babies. Beauty, however, is relatively static without glamour to spice it up. Glamour is everything you do to your beauty—the scarves you wear, the scent you wear, and the clothes you choose. *How can you make beauty part of your glamour toolbox to achieve your Great Work?*

Charm covers aspects such as wit, good conversation, and forging a bond with others, all things that are very useful in achieving your objectives. Beauty *is* and charm *does*. Charm can make you appear more beautiful to others than what's just on your surface because it's an outer manifestation of your inner spirit. Glamour is the spell you cast over others with your charm. *How can you make charm part of your glamour toolbox to achieve your Great Work?*

Organization is critical in glamour. Without organization, you will get stuck at the first stage of glamour (people giving you/buying you small things) instead of with a fully formed uprising for your ambitions. If someone shows you a business plan that is well-pitched, you will likely be more inclined to give a large sum of money than when someone says, "I kind of have this idea? Can I have five thousand dollars?" Glamour is the spark to inspire you to take a daydream into a structured plan. *How can you make organization part of your glamour toolbox to achieve your Great Work?*

Conviction gives you authority in your Great Work as it shows your passion and commitment to your cause. With conviction, you'll be able to see your aspirations through, even when you face failure and fatigue. Glamour gives you the strength of your conviction. *How can you make conviction part of your glamour toolbox to achieve your Great Work?*

You will need to be disciplined to be able to wield your glamour successfully. None of these aspects are easy to wield, but you must become adept at wielding them all individually and together. Think about your Great Work. How can you utilize beauty, charm, organization, and conviction (together and separately) to assist you? Remember, you don't have many resources as the oppressed and you will need to be able to brandish all of your carefully honed glamour tools in order to move forward. If you stop halfway in working toward your objectives, you will lose momentum and your efforts will become disempowered. You want to avoid this at all costs.

One
Small
Thing

All said about using glamour for more than trivialities, it's important not to discount glamour's usefulness in acquiring desirable trifles. After all, if you can't manage to be hand-fed bits of home-cured duck prosciutto like a tiny dog, how do you expect to unravel a kingdom? Make the beautiful boy behind the counter fall just enough in love with you that he puts extra *pain au chocolat* into your bag. Be witty enough that the person tending bar buys you a violet confection full of rose petals and crushed herbs. A sudden flirtation from your closest friend's wife. Suddenly all of your exes are eager to help you move. Your piano. Up and down three flights of stairs. Get the contract you need signed along with a wine-soaked dinner paid for by your client.

Your most secret, most coveted hungers aren't for anything as banal as a promotion with a minuscule pay bump or a slightly nicer car. You aren't employing forgotten cunning arts to accomplish something you could accomplish by merely paying slightly more attention to your surroundings. Figuring out how to be treated like a very low-level scene queen isn't your end game, your Great Work is.

However. Niccolò di Bernardo dei Machiavelli did not write *Il Principe* while living in his mother's house, eating sausage, and working for a bakery. He needed to be an advisor to Cesare Borgia, lead an army against him, lose the battle, be tortured, and then exiled to his country estate to complete his Great Work. If that small depiction of the whims of the Moirai frightens you into inaction, then perhaps your Great Work isn't as Great as you had thought. In the words of Machiavelli, "It must be considered that there is nothing more difficult to carry out, nor more doubtful of success, nor more dangerous to handle, than to initiate a new order of things."

Let us move on.

The First Piece of Your New World Order

Our first rite in actual glamour magic must be small. We must start with small things because without command over the small, there is no hope of ever gaining command over the grandiose. We will then weave together a tapestry of great and small acts of glamour until it is strong enough to become cloth. What may appear small on first reading may be enormous and vice versa.

Esoteric Experiment No. 5

Objective: Enchant an object to receive small favors.

You must select your object carefully. It should ideally be something new, something you can wear, something without previous energetic resonance on it. It does not have to be expensive, but it should be something you find beautiful. Something that makes you feel a sense of wonder. An evocative fragrance. A decadent lipstick. A shirt that fits you perfectly. Whimsical cufflinks. A flawless pair of shoes. Underthings that are completely flattering. A necklace with a sacred stone.

Once you have chosen your object and purchased it, select the date for your ritual. Chose a date that's powerful to you: A Friday because it's Venus's day. The date of the full moon because you feel your power swell during it. Saturday, July 23, because no one will be home in the house for the first time in months. Mark it on your calendar. Distill the favors you would like to receive into one sentence: I would like boys to flirt with me. I would like strangers to buy me cocktails. I would like shopkeepers to intentionally give me more than I purchased. I want to be praised for my beauty everywhere I go. I want others to tell me that I am witty and charming.

It must be simple, it must be a trifle that is easily parted with, though not always easily given. Whisper the date and your intention to your object every night before you go to sleep. Hold your object in your hand and stroke it as you would stroke a lover while you whisper to it.

When your chosen date has arrived, ready yourself for your ritual. You should be alone, which will allow your power to ebb and flow undisturbed by others' energy and pre-existing egregores. Every decision about your ritual should be approached mindfully as each decision will affect the outcome of your intended enchantment. Ritually cleanse yourself in your candlelit bathroom. Draw a bath full of rose petals, jasmine petals, and wild pinkster with frankincense essential oil. Use your most luxurious scrubs and washes to cleanse yourself of previous energies. When you step out of the bath, anoint yourself with warmed olive oil and myrrh. Consider whether you would prefer to be nude for your ritual or dressed. If you choose to be dressed, what will you wear to demonstrate your intent? What jewels will you adorn yourself with? Your feet should be bare.

Decide where in your home would be best to have this ritual. A room with a door that closes makes it easier to draw up energy. Contemplate which ritual tools would be best for this rite. A dual-bladed dagger. A chalice filled with cherry juice. Elemental representations. Images and offerings to your goddesses and spirits. Bee propolis incense on a censer. A spirit board. Heaps of roses. A cordial glass full of St. Germain. A teacup full of dirt from sacred places. A small decanter filled with your blood, your spit, your vaginal fluids, your semen. Your chosen object.

Seal the door shut with rose water, using a sigil that is protective to you. Seal any mirrors or windows with the same sigil. Arrange your selected objects. Begin to raise energy by chanting, singing, drumming, or dancing. Once you feel that you have raised enough energy for your Working, invite in your goddesses and spirits if you so desire. Tell them what offerings you have selected to give to them and why. Ask for their presence and assistance. Hold your object close to you. Breathe into your object until you feel your object's spirit stir and awaken. Anoint your object with your chosen fluid(s). This will be what you feed your object's spirit regularly, so make your choice carefully. Whisper your desire to the object's spirit. Put on your object. Look for an omen if you wish. Dispel the energy you have raised if you are inclined to do so by putting it back into yourself, into your object, into the earth or by unsealing the room, otherwise it will naturally dissipate over the coming days.

Wear your object regularly and continue to feed it and whisper your intent to your object's spirit until your intent is filled. Be prepared that it may take several weeks or even months and it is much like how a watched kettle never boils. The more you watch it and obsess over it, the less it will work. Watch and observe out of the corner of your eye and brain—that's where most glamour takes place. Do not move on to the next experiment until this experiment is fulfilled.

Once you are able to successfully regularly complete this experiment, it's important to remember not to get completely sidetracked by it. Being petted and fêted can be distracting to even the most intensely focused of us, as many of us are unused to it. Keep your eye on your Great Work and move forward.

Historical Glamour

Glamour is used to subtly influence situations. Nothing demonstrates this more than examples of historical riot grrls. These women weren't even considered *people* during the Middle Ages and the Renaissance, which meant that owning land and having money and agency over their bodies was incredibly uncommon. While most of these women weren't likely actually practicing Witchcraft, it sure didn't stop most of them from getting accused of it, and it didn't stop some of them from dying for the Craft.

What would you do if you had a Great Work burning inside you and you weren't even considered a person? You would use glamour, of course. It would be the only method available to you to accomplish anything. It would have to be subtle, it would have to be delicate. These women *couldn't* directly start epic field battles to accomplish their Great Works. Their options were limited and they knew it. That never stopped any of them. Throughout the book, I will use examples of these women so you can see how women without direct means found their way to their Great Works.

Lest you think that all these horrors were committed hundreds of years ago and we are fully entrenched in a brave new world where we don't have to worry about these things, in America in 1972 women without husbands *still* couldn't easily take out loans, have their own credit cards, or have car insurance. Women in general couldn't have legalized abortions until 1973. People in general couldn't be in same-sex relationships easily until the last twenty years, and mental health issues were still often treated with involuntary institutionalization until the early 1960s.

While the current world we live in is far from perfect in civil rights and economy, we have access to far more rights (if not money) than these historical examples. If they could accomplish their Great Works using the subtle influence of glamour with no actual rights, what couldn't we accomplish with glamour in this place in history, even as Other?

Rose Red, Rose White

The question for the aristocratic families during the War of the Roses was never an issue of *Are you a Good Girl or a Bad Girl?* The War of the Roses would provide ample opportunities for you to be both in equal measure. Bloodied hands, conspiracy, accusations of Witchcraft, marriages of opportunity, betrayal, loss of fortune, house arrest, stripping of title and lands, uncrowning and recrowning, fleeing for sanctuary in Westminster Abbey not once but twice, claims of Witchcraft, a bastard lineage with royal blood, a single son birthed by a child bride in the wilds of Wales who was so far from the throne he was almost in another solar system, a secret alliance between enemies, and two dead child princes. It would be an excellent soap opera. But it's an actual history between two women, Queen Elizabeth Woodville and Lady Margaret Beaufort, and it's a tale of two frenemies who together founded one of the most legendary dynasties in Western European history, the Tudors.

Elizabeth Woodville was a very unlikely candidate for queenship. She had been married once and widowed with two small boys in an age when virgins were generally preferred for queenship, which is sort of hilarious given how obsessed with succession the Renaissance era was. You would think that having a proven track record is a plus, but I digress. Also distinctly not in her favor: while she was gentry (of noble birth), she was not of royal blood (family had been kings or queens for generations). Only one woman without royal blood had married a king before in the entire English history up to Elizabeth's time and she was not crowned queen consort. Jumping over the moon likely seemed more possible. She also came from a family of turncoats, which was also not popular, but it was hardly uncommon during this particular war.

Nonetheless, she was living in gentile poverty when she petitioned King Edward for her allowance that her mother-in-law was keeping from her. The legend says she did so by waiting under a many-boughed tree for the king and his men to pass by her. She must have known she would only have a very short time to plead her case. She was renowned for being a great beauty, which likely didn't hurt her cause, but she must have had a good bit of glamour to boot to get as far as she did. Perhaps she wore her best dress, perhaps she plaited love knots in her hair, perhaps she had a jug of wine to offer the king. Whatever strategy she actually employed must have been carefully thought out, making the best use of her wits, beauty, and glamour. The king was very much taken by her, so he secretly married her in her family's small country estate.

That part is actually not terribly impressive as he had a reputation of doing so (likely in order to lure women to his bed with the promise of not just respectable marriage, but a queenship as well) and is known to have done it at least once before with Lady Eleanor Butler.

Several months later, it was far more impressive when the king publicly claimed her as his wife and made her a full queen consort, despite plans to have him marry French royalty. Elizabeth Woodville's star ascended so quickly that it should be no surprise that she was soon surrounded by jealousy and envy.

In the ongoing battles for kingship, Queen Elizabeth's husband lost, forcing King Edward to flee the country and Queen Elizabeth Woodville to seek sanctuary in Westminster Abbey with her children. During this time, Queen Elizabeth Woodville's mother, Jacquetta, stood trial for the first of several times against accusations of using Witchcraft. She was accused for using the Craft to make King Edward fall in love with Queen Elizabeth. Whether or not Jacquetta was actually a Witch, if she had been found guilty at any of her trials, she would have been put to death in a brutal manner. Luckily, she always managed to be found innocent.

Eventually, King Edward returned and was able to regain his crown and rule for thirteen years before dying from a sudden illness. Queen Elizabeth Woodville had two sons with King Edward. She and her family attempted to retain rulership, but King Edward's brother, Richard, had her eldest royal son locked in the London Tower and quickly executed key nobles who opposed him. The queen must have known that her options were bleak at this point, but she did not sit on her hands waiting for someone else to tell her what to do. She fled in the middle of the night with her children and once again sought sanctuary.

It was only a matter of time, however, before the new King Richard took her other royal son, though Queen Elizabeth Woodville and her daughters remained in sanctuary. Soon, it became clear that both boys had been murdered in the Tower, though it is still a mystery to this day as to who ordered it done. Most likely, it was their uncle, King Richard.

In quick order, King Richard had Queen Elizabeth's marriage nullified as her husband had been pre-contracted with Lady Eleanor Butler. Pre-contract was considered as legally binding as a marriage at the time, so he could not be married to Queen Elizabeth while being married to Lady Eleanor, making all of her children bastards. Her lands were rapidly redistributed to King Richard's favorites, leaving her bereft of her royal sons, her husband, and her wealth.

For some, this is where the story would end. Living in disgrace in sanctuary, no longer politically relevant, powerless, and helpless. Queen Elizabeth Woodville knew better.

While Queen Elizabeth Woodville's story was playing out, there was another story unfolding in Wales. Lady Margaret Beaufort was of royal blood, pious, and educated. She was married off at twelve to Henry VI's half-brother, Earl Edmund Tudor, who was twenty-four. After being wedded and bedded, the battles for the War of the Roses broke out, and Earl Edmund Tudor was taken prisoner and died of plague when Lady Margaret was thirteen and pregnant. She gave birth to Henry Tudor but it was a difficult affair; she would not become pregnant again. At fourteen, she was married to Sir Henry Stafford. The marriage lasted for thirteen years until Sir Stafford was killed in battle. During this time, Lady Margaret's son fled the country with his uncle Jasper Tudor and lived in exile in France, as he was a (distant) contender for the crown.

While Lady Margaret was not known for her beauty, she was known to be very charming and intelligent, which is a glamour of its own. For Lady Margaret's final marriage, she strategically selected Earl Thomas Stanley, who had the biggest private army in England at the time. During her marriage to Earl Stanley, Lady Margaret conspired against King Richard and assisted in a rebellion. Shared hatred of King Richard was likely the tie that bonded our two frenemies together, at least to begin with. Lady Margaret's husband managed to convince the king that somehow, despite living in the same house together and being married to Lady Margaret, he had no idea about her rebellious plans and was totally ride-or-die for the king. Once the king was convinced of Earl Stanley's loyalty and his lack of complicity in Lady Margaret's plotting, he took all of her lands and wealth and gave them to her husband and placed her under house arrest. It is very likely that two savvy politicos like Lady Margaret and Earl Stanley were intentionally playing both sides to better their family's fortune.

During this time, all of the other likely heirs to the throne were slowly dying one way or another, from sickness, battle, or execution. While still under house arrest, Lady Margaret saw her opportunity to put her son Henry on the throne. Since she and her new bestest frenemy, Queen Elizabeth, had been bonding over how much they hated the king's face through secret letters exchanged by their mutual doctor, Lady Margaret took that moment to say something like, *Hey new friend! We both agree that King Richard is the worst in every way. Say, since he killed your sons, maybe we should try to get* my *son on the throne? Because then! He could totally marry your daughter and we'd be officially royal (well, royal again for you, of course) and of course best friends forever.* Queen Elizabeth was no fool; she knew Lady

Margaret was crazy like a fox and her husband had a huge army, so she replied with something like, *What a great idea, new friend! Let's do it!*

Shortly after that, Lady Margaret's son Henry managed to finally land in England with a decent military force (though smaller than King Richard's army), thanks to his doting mommy's plotting and planning. The final significant battle in the War of the Roses was to be played out at the Battle at Bosworth. Lady Margaret's husband had a military force of his own that was large enough to sway the battle either way. Earl Stanley, a grizzled military tactician himself, refused to commit his force one way or another on the battlefield until he had decided who would be the winning side, even though King Richard was holding his son for ransom, threatening to kill him. Once Lord Stanley made the decision to commit his troops to Henry's side, the battle was a decisive blood bath, with King Richard killed alongside many of his men. King Henry VII's historian claimed that King Richard's battle crown was found in a hawthorn bush and Earl Stanley crowned King Henry with the circlet.

Lady Margaret was then known as Milady the King's Mother and signed all her documents as Margaret R. (Margaret Regina), and Queen Elizabeth Woodville got to be the dowager queen; they married their children together as planned. Were it a story and not history, it would end there with everyone happy again and all loose ends neatly knotted. But really it ends with Margaret R. opting to have her bestest frenemy exiled to an opulent convent so she would not have to compete with her anymore.

Lessons from Liz and Marge

These two women would *wreck* a current presidential election, they were such political beasts. What's important to note for your Great Work is that they got as far as they did due to two factors: Using their respective completely different kinds of glamour to influence situations as much as possible and to gain and regain favor when they were in disgrace. Glamour does that—you can regain favor by the sheer force of your glamour.

They spoke sweetly when they needed to, they expressed regret where it was needed, they committed espionage on an as-needed basis, and they made sure they always had people who were sympathetic to their plight and could help them out of crazy situations. It would behoove you to figure out how to incorporate those practical aspects into your Great Work should it go off the rails. Also, they always had a plan but kept it loose. Queen Elizabeth would have never expected her brother-in-law to (likely) have casually slaughtered her two legitimate heirs. Lady Margaret's son's claim to the throne started out so distant, it may as well have been on a different planet. They both had a long history of passionately despising each other. There was no reason to ever think they would be able to plot their two children taking the throne together, founding a new dynasty, the Tudors.

Let's Get Uncomfortable

For your Great Work to achieve actual greatness, you need to get good at forecasting potential outcomes to any action you take to move your Great Work forward. Not simply likely outcomes for each action, but unlikely outcomes and unforeseen outcomes as well. This requires strategic thinking and glamoury. Let's start with strategic thinking. Before you take an action, do your research. Research is a broad word here, it can mean actual book research and it can also mean talking to people about their experiences and gathering verbal intelligence. Let your research first inform potential outcomes to your action. Next, you want to use this information to create a cohesive strategy, noting to yourself which information seems the most solid to the least solid based on the sources. Then, prioritize what needs to happen for you to take action.

Let's say your Great Work is to play music professionally. Your research in this case would be: Finding a venue that is friendly to the kind of music you play and then asking around about the owner of your first chosen venue. You'll want to know what the owner is like to work with, what the owner's reputation is like, and how and when they pay. Then, once you find out a little bit about the owner, you would start to go to the venue to gather your own impressions while starting to develop a relationship with the owner, using your glamour to make the owner interested in your music. Once the owner gives you an audition, you need to make sure you prioritize your actions leading up to the audition: you have a great piece to play for it that you have practiced, you have a style that reflects your glamour, you've been doing magic to push the audition to go the way that you want it to go, and you did all the practical work to ensure your piece goes well (enough sleep, resting your voice or hands, not becoming distracted by outside events, etc.) and then following up after with the owner. Potential outcomes of this could be: becoming famous, becoming famous for all the wrong reasons, blowing your audition, getting the gig but not getting paid, getting the gig and getting fired from your day job, landing a contract for your work, getting the gig and never getting another one, playing the gig and then blowing it due to a social faux pas, getting the gig and falling in love with someone you met there and then being sidetracked from your music, and so on. You need to have a general idea about what you would do in these situations that you can predict, and become proficient in predicting potential outcomes, as that will give you the most opportunities in your Great Work.

So what do you do about outcomes you can't predict? They could be desirable outcomes that you haven't even thought of or they could be terrible things you never saw coming. No wonder everyone wants to be a control freak about their magical workings! But tightly casting limits you from opportunities that you want but don't even know you want. So let's work on keeping it loose enough to give us as many options as possible while working on our strategic thinking skills.

Esoteric Experiment No. 6

Objective: Cast a net wide enough
to catch unknown opportunities.

Choose a night when the sky is clear. Outside, make a small shrine using items that make you feel clear headed. Coffee. A spare pair of glasses. Running shoes. Your yoga headband. Your journal. Bring out a clear bowl filled with drinkable tap water. Draw sigils of protection onto yourself. Consider your Great Work and all of the outcomes you would like to come out of it. Imagine outcomes that you haven't considered that could be possible. Look up at the stars and draw lines between them using your finger to create a net. Think of this net as where your Great Work will catch positive unforeseen outcomes. Draw the net down from the sky into your bowl, either using a physical motion to do so or whispered words. Drink the water. Repeat this ritual until your net feels strong.

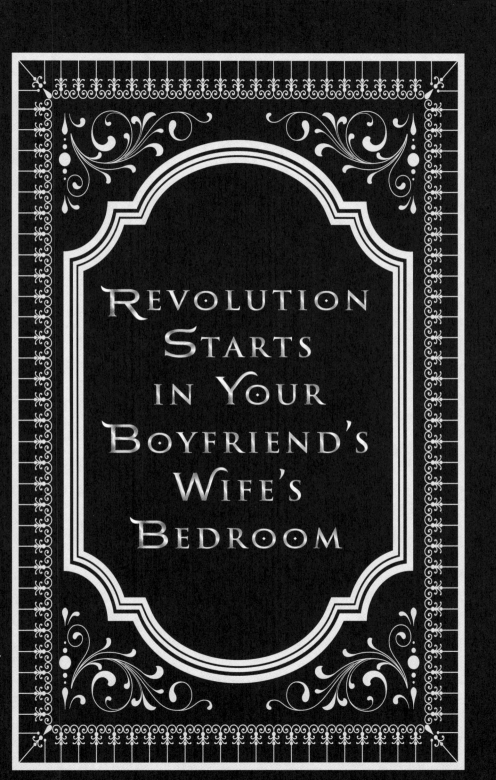

REVOLUTION
STARTS
IN YOUR
BOYFRIEND'S
WIFE'S
BEDROOM

Glamour requires beauty. Ironically, beauty is typically one of the first aspects to be deemed unnecessary when life gets hard, like we live in some kind of gray dystopian society. But why? In the Renaissance, beauty and art were considered important, and you were very likely to either die of plague or childbirth. When modern society talks about being "an ever increasing violent society," it's hard not to laugh. Elizabeth Báthory was only told to stop bathing in the blood of virgins when she started picking off princesses.

Public executions often happened in town squares for what would be considered either lesser crimes or not crimes at all by modern standards. Land war that would destroy your home as collateral damage was an aspect of daily life. And this was in the "civilized" societies. I digress. Life for most people has always been difficult. The world has been ending since it started. Why is it then that we are so quick to trivialize beauty in modern society? What are we living for if not for the beauty?

Glamour Looks Like You

When we start to discuss the external accoutrement of glamour, it's easy to get bogged down in what you think glamour *should* look like. Bond. James Bond. Joan Holloway, Queen of the Secretaries. While glamour does sometimes look like that, it's an oversimplification to constrain the whole of glamour Craft to the whims of the media. She is also equally proud to be Dr. Frank N. Furter, Motormouth Maybelle, Carrie Black,

Lloyd Dobler, Megan Beals-Botwin, Myrtle Snow, Hermione Granger, Hiro Nakamura, Clarice Jones, and Lafayette Reynolds.

Glamour is a demanding Craft to serve, requiring you to present your most exciting, beautiful self as often as possible, both to yourself and to the rest of the world. It takes a lot of work and dedication to be willing to do that. It takes courage to be willing to seduce yourself. If you can't beguile yourself, how do you expect to lure others into assisting you in your Great Work?

You deserve the opportunity to fall in love with yourself. Once you begin to consistently treat yourself like someone you love, beauty stops being optional. Would you deny your beloved beauty? A concert that sends her heart soaring? A book that spills tears down his face when you read it aloud to him? The most perfect cup of tea and lovely scones that makes them kiss you passionately when they see the table you laid out for them? Of course you wouldn't. Who doesn't feel reciprocal joy when their lover experiences beauty? Who isn't given a tiny gem of glamour from that shared experience?

So why do you forsake yourself, my love?

The concept of treating yourself like someone you love may sound like yet another half-assed post-feminist (No. No. No.) attempt at making you buy Dove products, but it's a critical part of your revolution. We've discussed that we are Other. We also need to face that as Other, we are told that our worth is lesser every day in big and small ways. Don't identify as a gender? Outsider. Are you a person of color? Outsider. Is your body different than what your culture defines as beautiful? Outsider. Are you part of the QUILTBAG? Outsider. Oh, your socio-economic status is difficult? Outsider. Are you disabled in any way? Outsider. Are you a Witch? Outsider.

You are not One of Us, thus you will never be beautiful and of worth. You will never be welcomed at the table, you will never be good enough. Ever. If you were, you would fulfill your culture's standard of beauty. You would be white, of course. You would be born into wealth. Your spirituality would have a proper place of worship—preferably four or five houses in your denomination—in your town for you to be seen in. You would love the opposite gender. You would have an opposite gender. Your body would be perfectly shaped in every way. If you were meant to be allowed at the table like an *actual* person, you wouldn't ask so many questions and would do what was expected of you by your family, your spouse, and your culture. You would sit down and shut up.

How much have you internalized this toxic waste dump that we all have been stewing in together on a daily basis? Real glamour, real beauty comes from being firmly rooted in your power. It comes from knowing who you are and what you're worth, especially as Other. Beauty is fearsome and terrifying. It's not meant to be accessible, it's not meant to be linear. If beauty was something that could be easily defined and quantified, we wouldn't be so messed up from trying to achieve what's considered beautiful for a hot second in time. It's a waste of everyone's time and simply irritates all parties involved. Heroine chic is in for a couple years and then it's curves as far as the eye can see to be fashionable. Your body can't do both of those things. Your body *shouldn't* do both of those things. But yet we are told that we should, and so we twist and contort ourselves, trying to manage to fill other people's expectations of how we are supposed to look and just how much space we are allowed to occupy on a physical and energetic level.

Anne B. Focused on the Big Picture

Getting back to our Renaissance women as examples of how to overcome glamour-related issues in this modern life, Anne Boleyn is a great example for dealing with not meeting her current societal expectations of beauty. Instead she focused on her wit and her glamour to move from a mere unroyal lady-in-waiting to the queen who overthrew the Catholic Church and gave a new religious movement power and authority.

Prior to becoming Queen Catherine of Aragon's lady-in-waiting, she was becoming the It Girl in France with her sister, Mary, who was a famous royal mistress. Anne became known for her experience in the game of courtly love, as well as being known for her prowess in literature and music, and her talent as a dancer, all things that were highly prized in her time.

When she moved back to England, she set her sights on Henry Percy, who had fallen in love with her. He was to become the Earl of Shrewsbury, a very powerful position in England at the time. Unfortunately, the betrothal fell through when no one would give permission for the marriage.

Mary was soon ousted as King Henry's mistress, and Anne stepped forward while still serving Queen Catherine of Aragon, which is a brilliant *and* stone-cold maneuver. *Oh hi, Queen Catherine. Totes boning your husband. I'm going to steal him out from under you and marry him, which is a nearly impossible task, but one I feel up to! Good talk. Ready for me to dress you?*

Then, Anne Boleyn managed to be crowned as a titled aristocrat in her own right (given to her by King Henry) when she was made queen, despite the general populace hating her face for being nouveau riche and not Queen Catherine. She would throw down with Cromwell when needed and was known to be a power behind Henry VIII's throne. She gave birth to Elizabeth I, who was the first queen to rule in England without a king.

Naturally, since she had what could liberally be called "a problem with authority," that got her exactly where you would expect it to get her (a head shorter), especially since she had not produced a male heir. Trumped up charges about adultery and incest with her brother got her locked up in the tower for treason, though it is incredibly doubtful she was actually guilty as she was crazy like a fox and it seems very unlikely that she would have intentionally done anything to lose both her head and the throne.

Lessons from Anne B.

Now that you have the basics down about her, let's get to how this matters to you. One would assume that she must have been the height of what was considered beautiful during her era to have so impressively turned the Establishment upside down, especially if your primary source material is the television show *The Tudors,* where she is portrayed by Natalie Dormer, who is also the epitome of what our current society considers beautiful. Naturally, much of the documents of Queen Anne's time were full of reports of how hideous she was, but Anne had a…tumultuous relationship with most diplomats so they were a bit biased against her. Then of course, there were reports from people who wanted to be in favor with the king so her beauty was extolled to conventionally beautiful heights of her time.

The truth like with most truths is likely somewhere in the middle. Queen Anne was likely no great beauty; she was likely fairly ordinary looking with brown hair and olive skin, neither of which were considered beauty traits of her time. Her eyes were said to be compelling and she was known to be fashionable and clever. No doubt she made the most of what she had in both arenas, creating a glamour about herself that lives on to be continually part of our literary and dramatic landscape to this day.

Now, all this having been said, do you think that it was more important for Queen Anne to be conventionally beautiful for her time or for her to convince King Henry that she was the greatest beauty he had ever seen by using her glamour, her wit, her cleverness, and flirtation?

Occupy the Space You Stand In

It is incredibly difficult to take up space when you are Other. We are taught to shrink ourselves and apologize for being flawed, aged, not a certain size, or any other many reasons you can think of. But that's exactly *why* we need to take up space. You are entitled to the space your body occupies but more than that, you are entitled to define beauty as you want to define it and not apologize for either of those things. Once you can really become comfortable with internalizing those statements and synthesizing them on a body level, you will be able to understand that the true underpinnings of glamour aren't about how symmetrical your face is and how committed you are to your culture's standard of beauty but becoming present in your body in its current form and using glamour to shape how you present yourself to the world at large.

Esoteric Experiment No. 7

Objective: Lessen your baggage about external beauty and enchant beauty into yourself.

Select a ritual space that has a sink. Arrange your ritual objects. A large ornate bowl. Your best chipped teapot full of hot water. Your softest towels. A beautiful vintage scarf. A cauldron with Epsom salt and alcohol. A small stack of joss paper and a black marker. Matches. An eyeliner pencil in your color of choice. A plate that once belonged to your showgirl great-aunt heaped with dried hibiscus, chamomile, and rosemary. Beeswax taper candles in mismatched holders. A small jar of cocoa paint you have created. A paintbrush. Graven images of your goddesses and spirits. A large mirror.

Seal your space by placing salt over the threshold of the room and then pressing your tongue to your index finger and pressing it to each wall in the room with the intention of creating sacred space.

Purify yourself by writing or inscribing any damaging thoughts you have about your physical form on the joss paper. Light your cauldron fire. Let it all burn away. Focus your intent on the fire purifying yourself from these unhelpful thoughts.

Take your clothes off. Sit in front of the mirror gazing at yourself. Continue to stare at yourself past the point of comfort. Continue staring at yourself until you only have kind words and intentions for yourself. Use the eyeliner pencil to inscribe your mirror with seals and symbols that are sacred to you and your path to your desperate yearning. Gaze upon yourself through the inscribed mirror until you feel your power rising within yourself. If you need an extra push to get into a sacred headspace, chant, visualize, or imbibe an intoxicant until you get there.

Pour the water into the bowl and put a drop of your saliva into it. As you pour the water, also pour your intention into the bowl. Breathe on your herbs until you feel them stir with life and add them to the water. Shroud yourself over the bowl with your scarf or towel, focus your intention on taking beauty into yourself as the perfumed water enters into your skin.

Scry using the water until you see how to use your beauty as a tool to obtain what you have been longing for. When you know the answer, seal it into your body by painting words, glyphs, sigils, and illustrations onto your body with your cocoa paint and brush. Sit with your intention until you feel you know what actions to take both magically and mundanely. When you are ready, wash the paint from your body.

RITUAL COCOA PAINT

¼ cup plain Greek yogurt

1 tablespoon quick oats

2 tablespoons cocoa powder

1 tablespoon honey

Mix everything together.

MIRROR,
MIRROR

You are beautiful. Right now. You are worthy of glamour. You are worthy of beauty. You are worthy of love. If you can't internalize that, think of the words of RuPaul: "If you can't love yourself, how the hell you gonna love someone else?" If you can't internalize that you are worthy of love, beauty, and glamour, how will anyone else? There is this pervading myth that if you care about how you appear, you are vain and vapid. Life is so full of drudgery, so very full of dishes, filing, going to the grocery store, and keeping your life afloat. Why would you deny yourself the opportunity to take pleasure in a sexy pair of stockings, a well-tailored jacket, lovely leather boots, or whatever floats your fancy? Is it because you have feelings about all of this?

You're Not Shallow, You're Motivated

Some people feel very put-upon about having to work at their appearance; that it is something they should not have to be bothered about. You know what's sexy? Your brain. You know what else is sexy? Your meat suit that it's currently encased in.

I don't look like what the media says is gorgeous.

Fuck the media.

I don't know how to feel beautiful.

We are going to change that right now.

True glamour isn't about putting on a costume. It isn't about conforming. It's about what do *you* think is beautiful? If you had to go to a party

63

tonight at the last minute, is there something you could pull out of your closet and feel immediately wonderful in?

Do you feel like a fabulously fat Audrey Hepburn when you wear pearls? Then wear them. Do you feel like a decadent Jamie Dornan when you wear a certain scarf? Then wear it. Do you feel like Eddie Izzard and/or Tilda Swinton when you wear your favorite pair of sunglasses? Then by all means, wear them.

If you are having difficulty with accepting your physical form as it is right now, reframing is a good place to start. The purpose of reframing is to take current negative thoughts that you are having and change them in your mind so the way that you see yourself slowly starts to change. For example, I am very self-conscious about my upper arms. You will rarely see a picture of me wearing something sleeveless. Even when I try on clothes, I am sure to have a cardigan with me so that I don't disregard flattering clothing because I'm too busy staring at my upper arms. It's something I'm still working through, but I started to make actual progress about being willing to accept my upper arms when I started reframing how I thought about them. Instead of thinking things like, *ugh, my upper arms are fat and hideous and look like bat wings*, I would instead remind myself that plump arms were admired in *Anna Karenina*, especially Anna's and she was a sex bomb. Granted, she throws herself under a train but still, she was dipping it and doing it. So I would think to myself that my arms are plump so that I will be hearty enough for the revolution.

The changing of your thought processes won't happen overnight; it requires constant mindfulness and you will sometimes slip, even with years of practice. All of this is okay, we're not looking for full body enlightenment here, we're simply working to be kinder to ourselves. Reframing has helped me be much more positive about my body and appearance. When I look at old journal entries from ten years ago, I feel my insides curl up like a pill bug because twenty-six-year-old Deb was just so *mean* to herself and it was *all the time*. I look at pictures of myself from that time and I have no idea why I was so full of self-loathing. I just didn't have the experience or self-knowledge yet to be kind to myself yet. All I could think about were all of the ways I was lacking, everywhere that I had too much or too little. Thinking all of these terrible things about myself was just such a waste of time and energy when I could have been learning to dress for the body I actually had—not the one I thought would magically appear one day, learning to wear makeup and do my hair in a way that would feel natural to me instead of ping-ponging between weight gain and weight loss and corsetry and eyeliner and pony tails and yoga pants. Knowing this doesn't make it any easier for any of us to stop, but we could be creating art, creating joy, creating wonder instead of concentrating on what we perceive to be imperfections.

It can be helpful to take a moment to see yourself through the eyes of someone else. When I was a nanny to an adorably wonderful tiny two-year-old girl, she would like to sit on my lap and then wedge herself directly into a roll of fat on my tummy. When she would do this, I would be inwardly dismayed. There's nothing like a small person curled directly into a place on my body that I felt super self-conscious about to really bring my attention to just how subconsciously displeased I was with it. But she was tiny and I was usually exhausted, so I would accept it. One day, she looked at me and smiled and patted my tummy approvingly as if to say, *thanks for this, lady! I enjoy lap time together because of your squishiness.* I would swat lovers' hands away from this area of my body, but when a guileless toddler was pleased with the shape of my tummy, it made it easier for me to accept that adult humans could be into it too. And if other people could love my body's shape, couldn't I do the same for my body?

A moment of indulgence: I have been dreading writing this part of this chapter. If I talk about appearance, the desire to distill such a complicated creature as glamour down to one aspect is almost unavoidable, even though beauty is merely one aspect of glamour. If I only frame glamour in terms of "Just be yooou, no matter what, in all circumstances, ever," you may be inclined to think that you simply need to accept yourself and the rest of the universe will fall in line with no additional work on your part.

Except ... no one thoroughly knows your innermost secrets, charms, and delights when first meeting you. They are not on display. Your appearance, your diction, your wit, and a small measure of your intelligence are, however. Lest you think it is simply the cruelty of our oppressors who indulge in this less desirable behavior, be aware that you (yes, you) are deciding how you feel about someone in the first seven seconds you meet that person, too.

If you want achieve your Great Work, you are going to need new influences. Dates, networking, job interviews, parties, conventions, and meetings—it will be impossible to move forward without at least some of these aspects. You will need to change the impression that some people in your life already have of you and make favorable impressions on people who will be newly entering your life. If you want to see real change in your life, you will need to be able to subtly maneuver people in your life who occupy places of power and privilege over you because that's how your war will be won. If you do what you've always done, you will get what you've always gotten. If you wanted what you already had, what's the point of accomplishing your Great Work?

Dress for the job you want to have, dress for the life you want to live? Yawn. Pass. Glamour will become immediately distracted by the girl in the tattered, faded vintage floral dress exuberantly running through puddles in purple kitten heels. If succeeding in your ambition was as simple as buying new clothes, wouldn't everyone have done that already? Wouldn't everyone be living the lives they want to be living?

Cultivating your own sense of style doesn't "just" happen. It requires conscious effort. It's easy to be dismissive of style; it's easy to gloss over this chapter as yet another makeover montage. If you are accomplishing your Great Work using glamour, you must be subtle. Clothes can be just clothes if you wanted them to be, but why would you not want to use them as a tool? Choose this scent to wear when you need Luna's influence, choose this color to wear because it is your nemesis's favorite color and you want to show him you can wear it better, wear silk because the goddess you are working with demands it, wear heels because your spirits say it will be a sacrifice, do your hair like your grandmother did because it makes you feel as bold as she was when building aircrafts for the war.

Glamour Doesn't Work Unless You Use It

If you are weaponless and about to enter combat and someone hands you a knife, are you going to throw it on the ground outside of the arena and say, "Hey thanks, I know my opponent has a crossbow and a horse and I've never been formally trained in combat or anything, but I feel good about going into this barehanded"? Because if that's the plan... I have to tell you, it's not good. If you keep looking at your appearance as optional, you are discarding a weapon from your arsenal. Use style as a weapon. Discarding weapons is a foolish decision. Don't be foolish.

Because glamour is something that is self-made instead of simply gifted to you, this is such a thrilling chance to present yourself however you like. Using glamour as an external expression gives you a chance to create something that *you* find lovely. It's not about being palatable to everyone who crosses your path; it's about taking up the space your feet land on.

It's choosing what *you* find sexy, what *you* find beautiful, and what *you* find powerful, even if no one else gets it at first. It can take a while for others to understand your chosen stylistic expression if it's outside of their comfort zone, and that can be difficult to power through. It's hard to be a trailblazer. It's frightening for everyone; it's scary for you to feel more perceived or perceived differently by others than you had previously, and it's daunting for other people you come across if they've never seen anyone like you.

But there are real-life workplace goth girls, pinup moms in the super-market, elder fashionistas with rainbow pastel hair at the concert, genderqueer fashion plates at restaurants, and impeccably dressed gentlemen on the subway. Obviously, if you live in a more conservative area or work in a conservative environment, it's going to take a very light touch to make this work and not turn your life into a disaster. This can be a delicate and difficult maneuver to figure out and may take some missteps to find the right place.

From my own experience, I hate wearing "corporate drag" which I personally define as: trousers, heels, a button-down top, a jacket, conservative jewelry, a full face of makeup, and hair that is carefully straightened every morning. For me, this sounds like a circle of hell. All that time, effort, and synthetic fabric. I love how *other* women look in it; Effy from *Skins,* Grace from *Will & Grace,* and real-life friends and coworkers. But for me, it feels like I'm wearing something that would somehow please my mother and not me—like my clothes are wearing me.

I started working for a conservative company recently and the idea of getting back to that made my skin crawl. With careful, slow experimentation, I have come to find that a retro/boho look with lots of sparkly jewelry is workplace appropriate, and I get a lot of compliments from both my coworkers and clients. I wear cupcake-like skirts, frilly little jackets, kimonos, and 1950s-inspired dresses with a bright red lip and my hair pinned up. Would I be able to "get away" with that if I didn't spend a lot of effort making it look polished and put together and presented a confident face while wearing these things? I doubt it. Would this work if my hemlines were not conservative and if my tops were low cut? It would not. Does it help that the only other person my age there shops at the same places? Yes it does, because that means this is what "young" people wear (. . . I work in an older environment).

Beauty Is Static, Glamour Is Magic

Beauty isn't something that can be changed all that much; dyeing your hair blonde isn't going to somehow change your bone structure, no matter what the beauty industrial complex tries to tell us. Does that mean that you shouldn't utilize cosmetics? The fallen angel Azazel gave us cosmetics to use, according to the Apocrypha. Are we here to create Witchcraft or make mud pies? Of *course* we should use whatever feels comfortable to us: cosmetics, hair dye, jewelry, clothing that would be worthy of sumptuary fines? Hell yes. Yes. But much like the first time you summoned a particularly exciting spirit, there are caveats.

First, you need to have a realistic expectation about what the use of your choice of products will *actually* do for you. Not what you want it to do or what the ad campaign's false glamour of their ad tells you it will do, but what it will actually do. Dyeing your hair raven black will not magically make your tummy flat, it will make your hair black. That's all. A smoky eye will put eye shadow on your eyelids, not remove stretch marks. A new top will not remove scars. Once you can get right with that, it's game on.

Not so fast though.

The second equally important caveat is something that many of us have learned the hard way: your credit card is not a natural extension of your income. Let me repeat that, because it took a very long time for that to really permeate my brain: **your credit card is not a natural extension of your income.** Maybe you desperately want a Hermès bag. It's a finely crafted purse, was a media buzzword for a while, is a status indicator, and may make you feel more glamorous. It will do none of those things if you can't pay your mortgage to get it. Does it mean you can't have one? No. It means you have to want one *very* badly. It means saving all of your change and giving up your other vices such as smoking, Frappuccinos, movies, take-out, and other such things for possibly a decade. If it is something you want that badly, then go for it. Do *I* think a handbag is worth that level of commitment? Not currently, and I am a well-known handbag whore. But you make your own decisions for yourself like a real, live adult.

Your Style, Curated

Part of developing a sustainable style is having a serious talk with yourself about what you can actually afford. If you can only afford to alter thrift store or freecycle items, that's fine. People will view it as a carefully curated look. Perhaps you closely check the stitching on clothing from Target and Forever 21 and you only buy pieces that look timeless and a very occasional "on trend" piece as well. Maybe you go to drugstores that have cosmetic testers so you can be sure to pick the right shades for yourself. You will look effortlessly chic. Perhaps you can afford to splurge on an occasional good leather handbag, shoes that were made to last, a cashmere wrap, and a consulting session with a beauty specialist. You will look put together and stylish.

At the end of the day, most people (unless they are fashion geeks), can't tell the difference between this season and last season. They are looking instead to see how well something looks on you. People who don't want to associate with you because you are working to not acquire an epic level of debt to keep up with people outside of your income bracket are not people you want touching your Great Work anyway. Fashion geeks who can tell if you are wearing something that is currently in fashion or bought on sale because it's last season, are still looking to see if it looks becoming on you. Nine out of ten times, they are not getting together with all of your other friends to judge you—they mean it when they compliment you.

Speaking of compliments, if you want glamour to work, get good at gracefully taking a compliment and not dissolving into an apologetic pile of self-loathing. You don't have to return a compliment with a compliment; in fact, in most cases don't. Wait until you sincerely mean it and it's not complimentary quid quo pro. The compliment scale will balance. If you give a compliment first, be sure to mean it sincerely and not expect anything back, as this will build a truer bond between you and the other person.

And finally, if you are worried that others will think you are putting on airs or somehow not being yourself by paying attention to details or if you are in a relationship with someone who wants you to dress or not dress a certain way (ditto for makeup and other products), that is actually the last barrier between you and your fully realized feminist self. *Choosing* to wear—or not wear—any particular piece of clothing or cosmetic is a feminist choice. Allowing someone else to dictate the way you present yourself to the world outside of the workplace (because earning a living is important) is not a feminist choice. At the same time, wearing something on occasion because it makes your partner happy is a choice you are entitled to make. Permitting someone else to dress you like you are a toddler in a non-consensual kinked scenario is not.

What kind of clothing do you like? Why do you like it? How can you make yourself feel delicious while doing dishes? What could you wear to bed that makes you feel scrumptious? What could you wear that would make you feel powerful and in control in your workplace? Does fabric matter? Does the country it was manufactured in matter? What is your budget? Do you own everything you need already? If not, where can you go to buy items that are within that budget? What do you wear that makes you feel crummy about how you look? Could you get rid of what makes you feel crummy? If not, what could you add to it to make you feel better about it? Accessories? Sexy underthings? Tailoring?

If those questions make you feel cast adrift, consider hosting a clothing swap. There's something genuinely magical about connecting with friends and friends of friends and stepping outside of your comfort zone and trying on clothing because someone says, *I think you would look great in this.* It gives you an opportunity to play in an environment that feels safe (these are your friends, so they already love you) and it's a way to experiment with a new look without having to invest actual capital in it.

Your (External) Glamour Checklist

1. Do your clothes and shoes fit properly? If not, there are lots of online tutorials to teach you how to fix that without owning a sewing machine. There are also lots of tailors and cobblers who are happy to take your money.

2. What condition are your clothes in? Lint rolling your clothing in the morning is a good first step. Polish your shoes if they need polishing, iron your clothes if they need ironing. Make repairs as needed. Do you wear clothing that cannot be salvaged due to irreparable wear and tear? Can you replace those items or make do without them?

3. Do you know what will look stylish on you? If you are struggling with this point, you can never go wrong with basic black. Kelly Cutrone is a fashion PR maven, and she wears almost no makeup, never does anything much with her hair and she always wears a well-fitting but nondescript black outfit with her signature *try saying something about my appearance, I dare you* stare. Black top, black bottom or black dress, black shoes, black wallet, and/or handbag, black socks or stockings, done.

4. Do you drink enough water every day? It makes a difference in your skin.

5. Do you take care of your skin? Cleansing and moisturizing is good for every skin type. If you are not sure what to use, talk to someone knowledgeable at a shop like Ulta or Sephora.

6. Have you been to the dentist in the last six months? Teeth are an indicator of social status in modern society. If they are stained or missing, that's part of what makes your first impression. Dental cleanings are often available at a discount from dental schools or Groupon.

7. If you have a beard, do you take care of it by washing it with shampoo and conditioner? Do you put a little oil in it so it looks shiny and healthy? Shiny, healthy hair is also a social status indicator.

8. How does your breath smell? Ask someone who will be honest with you, such as a parent, spouse, sibling, or lifelong friend. If it does not smell good, that's going to be problematic. Check with your dentist about what can be done. Remember to brush your tongue and the roof of your mouth with your toothbrush.

9. Do you style your hair? If your hair looks messy or unpolished, it detracts from making a positive impression. Again, the Internet is full of tutorials for the challenged.

10. Do you wear makeup? If so, put on some (noticeable) lip gloss and some tinted moisturizer for daily wear if you are unsure about what to wear.

11. How is your posture? People who sit and stand up straight are perceived as more confident. We are working to attract helpful influences for our Great Work. This will help with that.

12. You want to look polished and put together because it's an easy way to make yourself believe you are capable of the sweeping life changes you want to make every time you look in the mirror. It's the also the first step to charming others into getting on board for your cause.

Optional Social Experiment No. 2

Objective: Be treated the way you would like to be treated by others using your style as a weapon.

Before you overhaul your style, keep a photo journal of what you wear for a week. Take notes every day about how you are treated by others. The following week, once you've created your style for yourself and you are following the checklist, observe how others treat you then as well. Is it different? You want to pay special attention to how you styled yourself when you are treated the way you want to be treated. How did you feel about yourself each day? If you feel good about your style and you are being treated the way you wish to be treated and it helps your cause, then you have successfully created a new tool for your arsenal.

Developing *Kosmesis*

In Greek mythology, queens, goddesses, and demi-goddesses would perform *kosmesis,* the art of dress and adornment. In the *Iliad*, Hera decides she's going to seduce her husband, Zeus, so a particular battle will play out the way she wants it to. She has a full makeover montage where she bathes, puts on perfumed oil and cosmetics, braids her hair in the newest most fashionable 'do, and chooses the dress and jewels she knows will make Zeus desperate to get down with her. What better way to use your style as a form of magical glamour than to do something that goddesses and queens did to prepare for battle, seduction, or their current Great Work? Use kosmesis whenever making an impression is particularly important.

Esoteric Experiment No. 8

Objective: To perform kosmesis as a sacred
ritual to use your physical glamour.

Lay out your chosen outfit ceremoniously, including underthings and accessories. Arrange any cosmetics, moisturizers, hair tools, and accessories and fragrance at your mirror. Choose these items and your bathing objects based on your intent for the impression you want to make. Bathe, with your intent on how you want to present your glamour. Style your hair and cosmetics with your intention while gazing at yourself in the mirror until you feel confident in your intention and the impression you will make.

Your Glamour Needs to Be Active

Do you treat glamour like Pinterest? Pinterest is so seductive because everything is beautiful and nothing hurts there. Your friends pin the diets they will never start, the improvements they will never make to their homes, the crafts they will never do, the projects they will never complete with their children, and the newest healthiest recipe they will never actually cook. Everyone has a plan for the future that is bright with good choices that will never actually be made. It's easy to treat your glamour like a Pinterest board of good intentions and bad follow-through.

If my glamour worked the way the way I wanted it to, I would be dressed in a gorgeous silk dress that flows over my body like water. I would be at a party where everyone is beautiful and charming and wearing gorgeous things. We would be drinking wine out of chalices and eating fresh figs and we would all be as witty as Dorothy Parker and Oscar Wilde. We would dance, we would cavort, and then I would sprawl over the table and my party guests would close the table up into a makeshift boat and lead a procession to float me out onto the lake like an Arthurian legend. Does this description sound familiar? It's a Florence + the Machine video for their song "Rabbit Heart (Raise It Up)" and bears zero resemblance to the life I actually live. My body is not suited for silk gowns, my friends aren't constantly entertaining, and I don't actually own any chalices.

It could be argued that I could construct my life to be more accommodating to this glamour fantasy. Surely, I could scrape up some chalices at some thrift stores, I could have an outdoor party, I could have more interesting conversations and get some silk gowns altered and maybe I could work on the boat choreography (maybe), but even if I did all of that, it can't be my life all the time.

Laundry needs to be done, one can't live solely off of figs and wine (... I think). Books and blogs need to be written, yarn needs to be spun, candles need to be poured, milk needs to be bought, tax documents need to be processed, phones need to be answered. The bigger challenges are, how can you find a moment in your day that feels like your idealized version of glamour so that you can feed your glamour magic properly? How do you reconcile your Pinterest version of glamour with your actual blood-and-spit glamoury? How can you be true to your glamour in your actual life that you are living now while still working to fulfill your heart's desire?

When in Doubt, Ask a Goddess

Reconciling your idealized glamour with your daily glamour is a difficult task, as is your Great Work. In these tasks, along with fully realizing your glamour, it's completely okay to ask an adult for help. By an adult, I mean your goddesses and spirits that you already work with. It's tempting to want to stay in the mindset that each goddess and spirit does a few specific things and nothing else, but that's really limiting, isn't? It's more productive to see your goddesses and spirits more similarly to how you see actual people. Your sister isn't just good at being a mom and doing dishes, she also could sell ice in the dead of winter during a snowstorm, is an *amazing* karaoke performer, and knows the words to every Brat Pack movie by heart. Your sister isn't just Person of Mom-ing and Person of Doing Dishes, she has lots of other things she's awesome at. Now, this doesn't magically make your sister good at things she's *not* good at. You know she's terrible with social situations; you know she's never been a lawyer before. Just because you really need a social maven and a lawyer right now is not going to make your sister suddenly able to do those things for you, no matter how much she may want to actually do those things for you. You need to look at your relationships with your goddesses and spirits and communicate with them using whatever methods you usually use and figure out who is a really good choice for what. Remember—just like people will sometimes oversell themselves to get a job, some goddesses and spirits will do the same too. So start small. It's also key to keep in mind that you are still asking for a favor, no matter how well or poorly they perform it. Again, treat them like people. Be appreciative, and if it's best in your relationship to offer a quid quo pro arrangement (If you do x for me, I'll do y for you), do that. It's also okay to throw your goddesses and spirits a totally fabulous party with offerings and praise and then say, "So..." Just remember, much like with people, if you never throw them a fabulous party without asking for something, they will eventually be onto you. So in between, be sure to make regular offerings. I would define a "regular" offering as praise, chat about your life, candles, fresh water, incense, the first bite of your dinner, and so on; things that don't cost much but are appreciated.

It is very tempting to want to strike up a new relationship with a new goddess or spirit who is known for glamour or luck or whatever you're working on. Sometimes, that's the right choice. Maybe your goddesses and spirits are all really not into glamour or deadlines and don't want to be bothered with it. Maybe your goddesses and spirits have done everything they could do for you and there's nothing else they can do and you still need more help. These are situations where it may be beneficial to get to know some new goddesses and spirits. But just like in life, your best choice is to start with goddesses and spirits who are already invested in you. It's the difference between asking a friend for ten dollars and a stranger.

Before starting a new relationship with a new goddess or spirit, remember that just as you have a choice about working together, so do they. A lot of times people mistake goddesses and spirits for gumball machine who can't wait to give you candy instead of beings with their own thoughts, feelings, and agendas. This means sometimes they are just not that into you. Take St. Expedite. Most Hoodoo practitioners swear by him. He gets shit done—fast. He likes rum and pound cake; sounds like a party guy. When Jow and I first learned about him, we were so excited. He's quick and motivated. Other friends of ours like him and he likes them. We got out our little shrine to him, made him offerings, put on our best new friend smiles, and poured him our best rum. We gave compliments. We didn't ask for anything, just tried to make a connection.

We waited.

And waited.

And waited.

We tried calling again. Maybe he didn't get our message. *That happens, new friend; we understand. Call us!*

We waited.

And waited.

And ... nothing. He didn't want anything to do with us. We were indignant. How could new friend not like us? We are incredibly likable—we were polite and nice. We tried to talk about crap that new friend would find interesting. New friend likes our other friends. How could new friend not like us? *We would be super awesome friends, new friend!* We don't really know why still, just like how at a cocktail party you don't really know why someone won't warm up to you. We weren't desperate per se. We weren't asking for anything, we weren't in dire straits. We just wanted new friend to be pals with us. Not everyone's going to like you in this life or in the spiritual life. C'est la vie!

When inviting your potential new friend over, treat them like you would treat a person potential new friend coming over for the first time. Make an offering that you think would impress potential new friend, make some good conversation, and don't ask for anything yet because that's weird and off-putting. See if you feel there's a connection. Invite potential new friend over a few times while making offerings and conversation. Be sure to know what potential new friend likes and does not like. Just like you can potentially offend a person potential new friend, you also have plenty of room to offend spirit potential new friend. Offended doesn't always mean they will wreck your house just like physical people don't often do that (but we all have *that* friend); sometimes they will simply leave in a huff or give you the silent treatment or quietly unfriend you. Give yourself some time to make a connection, ask for an omen if they are interested. See what happens and go from there. It's important to remember that what potential new friend thinks is good for you may not always match what you think is good for you; what potential new friend asks for may not be something you want to give, New friend is not obligated to always tell you the truth, and new friend may *seem* like a really good new friend but turn out not to be. If you no longer wish to be friends with new friend, slowly, gently, and politely back away. If new friend is not getting the hint, get your current goddesses and spirits involved.

Here is likely where you are expecting a Google contacts list of potential new friends for you to text and become Facebook friends with so you can network with them, like their statuses, and have them on deck just in case of a glamour emergency. That would make your life much easier, right? Am I giving out the names of my person friends to you for you to bother? No? Same applies here, friend! Do some research, do some magic, make those connections for yourself. Feel free to ask your goddesses and spirits as well as your person friends for introductions and connections! That's how your regular life works; that's how your magical life should work too if you ever want to get anywhere.

Esoteric Experiment No. 9

Objective: Reconcile your idealized glamour with
your daily glamour. Be the change you want see.

This experiment should take place in a bathtub if at all possible. Use water that is hallowed and inscribe a circle around your tub. Choose what will go into your bath as though it were a cauldron in which you will be remade. Oils. Perfume. Glitter. Dried flowers. Light only one candle on your vanity or sink and wear your best robe. Before drawing the bath, consider everything your glamour could be if actual life wasn't a hindrance. Take some soil that you have gathered from a place you find irritating and put it into a vessel that you have always disliked and rub your hands in it. Wash your hands with salt, lemon, and soap and wash the dirt off of your hands and watch it drain down your sink. Concentrate on letting go of your previous vision of your glamour as the dirt leaves your hands.

Disrobe. Start drawing your bath while singing a song that is sacred to you. Offer your goddesses and spirits a tray of treats that they would like. A glass of champagne, a perfect piece of dark chocolate, a sliver of truffle over pâté, fresh bread, incense, flowers, a perfume, cosmetics, a book, a fur mouse. Whether your words are simple and austere or floral and elaborate, use what comes from your heart place to invite your goddesses and spirits to join you, and then say out loud what you are offering to them and ask for assistance in your glamour.

Shut the water off when your tub is full. Concentrate your will on making the bath a welcoming place for your goddesses and spirits to communicate with you. Remember, "communicate" is a broad word for working with goddesses and spirits. Communication isn't always voiced words—sometimes it's a lyric, bibliomancy, a sound, a smell, a taste, a vision. Step into the bath. If you receive no communication as the water is cooling, drain a bit off and add more hot water. Concentrate on journeying inside yourself to your inner temple, a place where it is safe for you to receive visitors. Politely ask your goddesses and spirits to visit. If your house is still empty and there is no communication, keep doing this ritual every night until you receive communication about working on reconciling how to make your daily life a place for glamour.

Do divinations, record your dreams, look for omens, and ask for your goddesses' and spirits' help in your Great Work. When their suggestions assist you, be sure to show the proper gratitude. Never, ever make promises that you cannot keep to them. Never, ever make vows that you cannot keep to them. Never, ever promise offerings you cannot give to them. Much like breaking faith with a human lover/friend/family member can sunder your relationship in twain, the same will be true here as well. Breaking your faith with them could cause them to refuse your presence, muddle your Great Work, and turn fortune's wheel against you until you are ground under it.

Take It Off, Slowly

When attending *The Rocky Horror Picture Show*, the most exciting part is Dr. Frank's entrance into the theater. The audience starts stomping their feet to the click of his heels and regulars crane their neck to the back of the house to try to get a glimpse of who will be playing him. The role asks a lot, as most of the roles in *Rocky Horror* ask. The wig, the panties, the corset, the stockings, the heels, the vampy lipstick, all in front of a room full of people that likely include strangers, friends, lovers, exes, and possibly family members. No one wants to see a nervous, shy Dr. Frank, even if that's how the actor is feeling in the moment. When he whisks off his cape to reveal his full ensemble, he only has one moment to do it right. When done correctly, the whole audience screams and applauds in delight. When done with inhibition, well, everyone claps politely and hopes that Eddie will at least be able to dance with Columbia with aplomb because otherwise why bother seeing *Rocky Horror* live?

Gypsy Rose Lee didn't start her career in burlesque. She was a song and dance girl who seized the opportunity to become a show girl when one of her straps slipped one night and she started pattering with the audience about it. Her patter was so good, she was featured in a mainstream movie, *Stage Door Canteen,* performing a piece of it while doing a very G-rated strip tease. While Gypsy Rose Lee was very beautiful and talented, her glamour wasn't in her body, it was in her ability to keep everyone's eyes on her, even while she was still fully clothed, through witty monologues, facial expressions, glittery costumes, and her presence. Having command of her audience allowed her to decide when, how, and what to reveal to her spectators.

Part of what makes you interesting and exciting to others is in how you reveal yourself, in action, in conversation, and physically. The way you dress, when you tell a lover that you are in love with her for the first time, a long sloe-eyed glance with a stranger, how you tell a story about yourself, how you treat others, all of these tiny components make up your glamour.

What to reveal and when is not something most Americans spend much time thinking about. Until I started reading books about French women's *je ne sais quoi,* I didn't think about it ever. After all, I'm a blogger; I vomit up intimate details all the time for the whole Internet to silently judge me with and find me wanting all the time. But typically and generally speaking, in American culture, how fast one shares intimate details of one's life is a mark of how interested you are in each other as friends or lovers. While this often starts out in an exciting sort of manner *(You like pie? I like pie! You like cute animals doing cute animal things? I like cute animals doing cute animal things!),* this is not an unflawed process. Usually, when you feel like you've known someone forever in the span of two weeks, you are also vomiting out innermost secrets and traumas. Sometimes, yes, that can form bonds that last a lifetime.

Is This Relationship Serious?

But the issue here is that *feeling* like you've known someone all your life and *actually* having known someone all your life are two different things. When it's a feeling, sometimes you may feel inclined to share more than you meant to and then find out disappointing aspects about this new person—they are an unrepentant gossip which means now everyone in your social circles knows this information about you, they are fickle which means that you had this close bond and have shared meaningful things about yourself only for the other person to lose interest and wander off with all your secrets never to return, or they have other less desirable traits.

If you hadn't been so blinded by what you wanted to see (every way you are similar), you may have instead taken things more slowly and shared your stories and secrets at a more sedate pace. Information is a precious commodity for a reason—once someone knows something about you, they can't *un*know it. You have trusted this person to carry your stories and secrets and not use them against you. Wouldn't it be better in most cases to wait to be sure the person can be trusted with these sacred things before throwing them in the name of bonding?

Coming back to my prized *je ne sais quoi* books, while it is highly unlikely that as Americans we would shield what we do for a living from potential new friends and lovers for several months for inexplicable French reasons, along with various other untranslatable French ideas about not needing to officially call anything a date, we should still consider some aspects of French home life while getting our glamour bearings.

You can make yourself a more interesting conversationalist about literature, local events, world events, art, and cinema to slow down on the personal information overload when meeting new people and with people you already know. Being a good listener never goes amiss, and it's true that people love to talk about themselves, so ask questions about their experiences or thoughts. When you do speak, speak clearly so you can be understood. It never hurts to have a few anecdotes about your recent life experiences that can be told to various social circles. Be sure to give the other people you're speaking with a chance to talk, too. Every issue or problem that crosses your mind doesn't need to immediately be held up for presentation to the world; you can take some time to think about it on your own first and consider how and to whom it could be presented. Every moment of every day does not have to be spent in the company of others; you can work to carve out some small niches to have time to yourself both to decompress from being viewed by others and to concentrate on accomplishing your Great Work.

A new relationship of any kind with someone is an opportunity for you to form bonds that could last years, possibly decades. It's the beginning of a journey that will unfold as quickly or slowly as you and the other party allows it. A slumber party atmosphere is highly enjoyable, but if you have told this new person everything there is to know about you over the course of an evening or even a month, what will you have to share in two years? Burlesque isn't terribly exciting to watch if the stripper has his clothes off in a pile on the stage in thirty seconds flat. At the same time, you need to do a fearless self-inventory about how skilled you actually are at burlesque. Gypsy Rose could take off her gloves in a half hour and have everyone enthralled just to watch. You are not Gypsy Rose, yet. How interested is the other person in you? Ideally, you want to leave an interaction with the other party wishing they had more time with you, not grateful that you exited.

If you know you will have an interaction with a new person, it could be useful to consider to yourself what you would be willing to share with the other party and why, as well as what should be saved for a later time.

Think about it like this: in most circumstances, it is very distasteful to hear about the horrors of the other party's exes on the first date. If that is coupled with discussion of financial problems, dislike about mutual friends and acquaintances, and expectations about *this* relationship, it is very likely that you will back away as quickly as possible from this other person and the whole situation. You want to avoid being *that* date.

More than anything, practice will help you figure out your burlesque aspect of your glamour. As we've previously discussed, your Great Work is highly unlikely to be accomplished without some new influences. An easy way to get some new influences in your life is to broaden your current social circles. This happens by saying *yes* to outside events more often. Shows of all stripes, travel, crafting circles, professional meet-ups, events in communities you are a part of, conventions, parties, festivals, and conferences are excellent places for you to take your show on the road.

You Have to Leave Your House for Glamour to Work

Before going to one of these events, consider what you would like to get out of the event itself. Do you want a sexy romp with a friend of a friend? Do you want to find all of the best things to eat and drink? Have interesting conversations? Do you want to make new friends and lovers ? Do you want to find out new information that can give you new experiences? Do you want to say yes to things you wouldn't usually say yes to? Do you want to wear clothing that you rarely get to wear? Will finding specific people or situations at this event further your Great Work?

Be aware that making no plans to achieve the things that you would find at these events could potentially leave you feeling unfulfilled. At the same time, even if you plan everything as carefully as a debutante's ball, you may still find that nothing went according to your plans due to being personally overwhelmed or other people's agendas being less stringent than yours. When your plans involve other people (which they often will), expect a certain amount of chaos.

It may help for you to broadly plan your event. If you start networking before the event through social media outlets, it may assist you in finding out what events could be of interest to you. In this day and age, it's possible to have a fully booked social schedule before you even go to the event for the first time. Dates, meet-ups, hook-ups, classes, and lunches with small groups are all easily accomplished through some charming and witty banter online. However, be aware of a few things.

Sometimes people (possibly you) are more charming and interesting on the Internet than they are in person. No one is (likely) trying to deceive anyone. Everyone has time to think of the perfect *bon mot* to share, and with the ability to erase possibly regrettable statements, everyone is able to show their literal best angles in their photos, those aspects of themselves they think will be most glamorous. Internet exchanges are a great place to explore possible ways to present ourselves to others. From a glamour perspective, it's the ultimate sandbox.

But great chemistry on the Internet can fizzle in person, and lukewarm interactions on the Internet can actually be sparks in person when there are hormones and visual cues involved. It's often a good idea to be open to the experience if you make plans with someone you aren't sure about because it could be amazing in person. In any of these situations, it would behoove you to have an exit strategy in case a great connection goes stale. But before you run like a frightened rabbit, if the conversation is going off the rails because the other person is not staying on topic, you can ask questions about the actual topic to bring the conversation back to it. This may make you less desperate to escape because you are on topic again and asserting some agency in the situation. But if escape is needed, there's the standard *I'm just going to get a drink,* which can be tailored to your event. *Oops! Two o'clock is that workshop about making wreaths out of human hair that I promised my friend I would go to with her. Got to go, so nice to meet you!* You can use other escape methods, too. Often, it's easier to exit a conversation if you focus on the other person and what they are saying, give verbal feedback that you've heard what they said and then make your excuses (*I'm so glad we got to catch up, I have to run!*). If you know this will be a conversation that you want to escape from ahead of time or sense that you will want to escape early on, give a time frame. *I really want to focus on our conversation, but I have x amount of time before I have to dash, just so you know.* If you are attempting a longer, slower disentanglement (especially to get rid of someone from your space), it's helpful to change spaces with the person. *Hey, I'm going to go grab a drink from the kitchen, come with me.* Spend some time in the new location together, being focused on what the other person is saying and then excuse yourself to a new space alone. *It was great talking to you! I have to make a call outside/in my room. See you later!*

As always, be sure someone knows where you are when meeting new people and be sensible so you don't end up in pieces in someone's freezer. If you don't have friends at the event, you may want to consider installing an app like Watch Over Me on your smartphone. Watch Over Me allows you to choose an event for what you are doing (walking home alone, taking a cab, going on a date with someone new, etc) and how long it should take. If you don't respond to the app when the time period is over, your GPS coordinates are sent to your designated safety contact. It also has an emergency button.

An event like this is short term, meaning just that—it's short. Be selfish, be selective. You can't always do that in your usual life, eventually the people putting up with you being a feral psycho while attempting to achieve your Great Work will eventually get sick of you being constantly selfish and "selective." (First communion family party with no booze *and* no bounce house? Pass.) You need your support network to ideally be supportive of your endeavor (the parts you want to share, at least) and be willing to listen to you snotting and crying about failing at life ad nauseam and occasionally shove crackers in your face. If you are *very* lucky, perhaps they will do a few of your dishes.

If you book yourself solid for the whole event, you deny yourself the opportunity to be spontaneous, and if you meet new people who are interesting, you won't be able to do anything about it. It's a very limited (and liminal) experience, so if you find yourself getting cornered by people who are not glamorous *to you* and are unlikely to be helpful to your Great Work as well, you need to extract yourself as soon as possible, not even necessarily politely in some cases because sometimes others are not great at picking up social cues.

It is very easy to burn yourself out at these kinds of events because you are having an excellent time and are excited to be around like-minded people. Maintaining self-care during these kinds of events is critical. Make sure you sleep at least five to seven hours. Eat regularly. Shower regularly. Take your medications. Drink enough water. If you start to feel completely overwhelmed, take a breather and read a book or take a nap and regroup. Try not to catch everyone else's germs: wash your hands often, don't eat anything out of common bowls or plates (chips, unwrapped candy, et cetera), and take vitamin C and zinc starting a few days before the event and ending several days after the event.

Serious Goth Face Is Not Always Necessary for Glamour

Glamour isn't always serious, not at events or in your everyday life. If you've ever seen Dita Von Teese on a daytime talk show to promote a new book or lingerie line, she's giving the hosts lessons on how to dance in a giant martini glass (as it is so likely to come up in everyday life) or another one of her daytime television friendly burlesque dancer skill sets. She's done it so often that she's very matter of fact about it and even a bit silly about how she explains how to execute this event.

Make no mistake about how playful she may be now, doing College Humor sketches about how to sexily eat a Lean Cuisine: she's still a mogul who got to where she is due to how she presented herself. If you woke up one morning and decided to become a stripper in the late 1980s where hair bands were king and Tawny Kitaen was considered the height of beauty and you looked nothing like the other girls, you may have slunk home and become an early elementary school teacher. Dita didn't. She walked into that smoky bar, surveyed the bleached blondes in bikinis dancing like they were in a music video and concluded, *No one else looks like me! This is great! I have a niche!* She built her empire from that point.

Dita's brand isn't diminished by her daytime television antics, and yours wouldn't be either. You don't have to be serious all the time—you don't have to create a façade that ignores whole pieces of yourself to pretend to be only pieces that are easier for others to swallow or show only pieces that you think will be taken seriously. But you *can* diminish your glamour by not fully committing yourself to whatever path you have chosen to take to express your glamour in the moment.

In method acting, you always hear the phrase *what's my motivation?* If you are sincerely committing to your character as an actor, you should have a motive for every line that comes out of your mouth. *I want to convince the other character, I want to lie so convincingly that I believe it myself, I want to seduce her, I want to win this argument.* You are trying to *do* something active with sometimes passive lines. If you only half-commit to your character, the audience only half-commits to your version of that character, leading to crummy reviews and a lack of future opportunities. You want the audience to be invested because that is how you get to keep acting. Glamour works very similarly. When you are interacting with someone else, what are you trying to accomplish? Are you building a friendship? Do you want the other party to think you are clever and winsome? Do you want the other person to know how accomplished you are? Do you want the other person to like you because you like him? Do you want the other person to help you with an opportunity? Are you bonding? Do you want the other party to find you sexy?

Think about someone dressed very attractively. Now think about that person wiggling around in those clothes like a toddler forced to wear an Easter dress and bonnet. It's not that the person is now suddenly unattractive, but that person has undermined her own credibility. In glamour *what* you do is less important than *how* you do it in many ways.

If you visit a friend and her house looks like a hurricane ripped through it but she makes no apologies and serves a full tea with all the proper sparkling clean accouterments, are you going to be busy silently judging her about her house, or pleased with the tea she is sharing with you while you shove scones down your throat? She chose to commit herself to serving tea properly over de-cluttering her house and she committed to not being concerned about your opinion of her house in its current state, which in turn likely will make you more committed to enjoying the tea and not noticing the state of the house.

Perhaps you made a mistake in your workplace. Which will be more charming to your employer? Sobbing, self-flagellating, and being wrapped up in it for the rest of the day, or a sincere apology, questions seeking clarification, and a small, clever, self-effacing remark as you get on with your day and re-immerse yourself in your work?

If you are on a date and spill red wine all over your white top, is it better to run to the bathroom in a fit of humiliation, or roll your eyes, smirk, and say, "This is why I can't have nice things," and then ask for club soda?

It would be amazing if glamour made you perfect at everything at all times and completely attractive to every other human you ever encounter in life, but a key component to glamour magic is that it offers a way to be graceful when a situation *doesn't* work out the way you intended. We laugh when cats accidentally fall off of something and then strike a pose as if they meant to do that, but we laugh because we find it charming and endearing that they are attempting a recovery to a mistake. It's always much better to attempt to recover a mistake in a way that is loveable to your witnesses rather than huffing and getting annoyed, or worse, denying that it happened, which in turn annoys your witnesses.

As humans we tell each other all the time that we all make mistakes, so own yours. It makes you relatable to others. If you occasionally seem like you need help because you are clumsy like a chick lit heroine or burn the roast and others find that adorable, then haven't you helped yourself in receiving support toward your Great Work?

Esoteric Experiment No. 10

Objective: Practice controlling your glamour.

Choose a place where you have never been and no one knows you: a café known for its perfect espresso, a wine tasting class, a convention or conference that is in an area of interest to you, an Airbnb in an adjacent city, a shop you are never quite brave enough to enter, a blind date. How do you wish to be seen by others in this venue? What aspects of yourself do you want to reveal to strangers in this new place? What aspects have you specifically chosen not to reveal to strangers? This is an important aspect of incorporating burlesque as part of your glamour. If a burlesque dancer shows something that she didn't intend to show (or worse, is illegal to show), she has lost control over her performance. Think about your previous work on what makes you glamorous. How can you work to make those aspects of yourself apparent to strangers? How can you unfold your glamour to others? Is part of it what you wear? The drink you order? How you flirt with a stranger? The aloofness you present while reading a specific book? A few amusingly sly comments you make? Do you want everyone to be blinded by the sheer force of your glamour or only a few specific people . . . or perhaps a specific person? Practice turning your glamour on and off at will by drawing it up and dispelling it, using whatever method you would use to draw up energy for magic and then dispelling the energy after your rite has concluded. Spend at least three days contemplating this, as being in control of your glamour is important for achieving your Great Work.

Once you have taken enough time to decide on a course of action, perform the ritual aspect of your rite the evening before the practical portion. Select a place to perform this ritual that is conducive for you to write: your office after hours, your kitchen table, your bed, a tiny table and settee. Dress simply in basic black. Select your sacred writing implements. Silk chiffon paper from Calligrane, a goose quill as white as milk with india ink, a calligraphy brush and black nightshade ink, a typewriter and linen paper, a handmade journal and your

best pen, your MacBook. Decide upon any other ritual imple-
ments you may need: a ritual oil heavy with juniper berries for
self-anointing, a candle you have dressed with the appropriate
herbs and oils, your favorite book for bibliomancy, sacred music, a
canvas and charcoal, quartz crystal points you have cleansed by the
light of the moon, an egg to cleanse yourself with, a shot of whiskey
in a favorite demitasse cup, the Golden Moth Illumination deck.

Draw your power up through yourself and slowly walk in
a circle surrounding your work area three times while inton-
ing compelling words of protection, forbidding spirits with ill
intention from your space. If words are not always your pre-
ferred method of communication, use what is: drawing, sing-
ing, dancing, or creating a token. Use your ritual implements
however flows organically for you. Write out your intention
or pour your intention into the paper and seal it with sealing
wax. Breathe into the paper to finish sealing your intention.

Keep the paper on your person for your adventure—your
pocket, your bra, your purse. On the day of your outing, be
mindful of all of your actions, as every small decision makes up
your larger glamour. Dress with intent. Speak with purpose. Use
your body language with care. Notice your unconscious gestures.
Are you revealing what you intend to reveal? Are you being
viewed in the light you intended to be viewed in? Once your
practical has been completed, break the seal on your paper and
spend some time reflecting if you accomplished what you set out
to accomplish. If you did not, don't despair. Rarely does anything
new work the first time. Try the rite again from start to finish in
a new venue for the ritual and the practical. Once it does work,
see what happens when you use it with people who know you.
That may take several attempts before you are successful, as they
will be less susceptible to your charms.

Glamour and Great Work: Halfway Point Check-In

1. Have you established what your Great Work is?

2. Have you stepped into your power as Other? How will you use your place as Other as part of your glamour?

3. Are you able to procure small favors from others by using your glamour?

4. Have you established a strong code of ethics for yourself to follow?

5. How have you used your glamour to make progress in your Great Work?

6. What steps have you taken both practically and with your glamour to make progress in your Great Work?

7. What goddesses and spirits have you chosen to work with for your glamour?

8. How have you resolved your "idealized glamour" to your "actual glamour"?

9. How will you use your glamour to move forward in your Great Work?

10. Have you developed a sustainable sense of style?

11. How will you use your glamour to present yourself to others?

12. How will you use your glamour in a new environment?

13. How will you use your glamour in a familiar environment?

No One Woke Up Like This

You cannot win a battle alone, even if your saints and spirits are guiding you, you hear the voice of God Herself, and you have a map of everything to do and everything to avoid. The Maiden knew this. She knew that if she wanted to reunite France as an illiterate farm girl during a time that women were still property instead of people, she would need powerful allies. Always the shrewd tactician, she knew that if she could find a way to get to the king, everything would fall into place. King Charles VII was unanointed, desperate, and constantly losing ground to the British and the Burgundians. His situation was dire enough that he would be looking for something, *anything* to give renewed hope to his followers. What could be more inspiring than Joan of Arc, a young country girl guided by God, her banner rippling in the wind, her armor shining in the sun?

First, Joan needed to get to Charles. It was not exactly a smooth journey to get to him; even in the Middle Ages, people tended to give you a wide berth if you had a really big idea and claimed to be guided by saints and angels. Joan persuaded her cousin to take her to see the captain of the garrison of her town to get her an escort to see the king. It was initially received about as well as you would expect. The captain told Joan's cousin to take her home to her father where she should be beaten for having ideas. It was a small town, though, and it's not hard to imagine Joan lying in wait to see the captain every time he went to the butcher, the baker, and the candlestick maker using the time-honored, teenaged tradition of persistence about her petition until he was too worn down to say no.

While Joan was working on the captain, two soldiers became interested in Joan's cause, especially when they found out her "Lord" that she kept referring to was not a nobleman but God. Joan told the soldiers something along the lines of *Of course I would rather be at home doing what women are supposed to be doing! I would rather be spinning and helping my mother like any good Catholic girl. But if God, the saints, and the angels say you need to save the country instead, you can't just ignore them, am I right, boys?* Which probably seemed reasonably plausible to them, especially since Joan must have practically glowed in the dark with glamour.

The two soldiers convinced the captain to give Joan a second audience. This is where Joan says to the captain, "Oh by the way, while there's no logical reason a farm girl should know this and this battle is happening in a place very far from here, let me give you an unlikely prediction about how this is going roll." Joan then correctly predicts the outcome of the Battle of Rouvray. After her prediction is confirmed by messengers, the captain decides he doesn't have much to lose at this point, so he suggests to Joan that she wear men's clothing to keep her from being raped on the road and sends her off to meet Charles with a small escort.

She eventually makes her way to court and is granted an audience with the would-be king. It is likely that Charles is persuaded to give Joan a chance due to predictions she made to him privately, but it was his mother-in-law, Yolande of Aragon, who financed Joan's campaign and confirmed her virginity and her title as "the Maiden."

Joan was then sent to the ongoing battle in Orléans where she took an arrow in the neck and survived. Once Joan arrived and the French were offensive in battle, the English retreated. This persuaded the Duke of Alençon to accept Joan's advice, which assisted him in winning the battle in Jargeau. Troyes was taken in a bloodless siege and shortly after that, Charles was crowned. Joan never participated in active battle herself; instead she carried her banner for her army.

Eventually, Joan was captured by the Burgundians and held by Joan of Luxembourg's family. The countess and her ladies were immediately won over by Joan's charm; they treated her well, though she was not the easiest of prisoners to hold on to. At one point, she swan dived out of her tower into the moat to attempt to escape. Soon after that, she was sold into English custody. Though Joan was imperative to Charles's rise to kingship and the support he received, he chose not to exchange her for an English prisoner of comparable worth and instead accepted approximately the equivalent of USD $100,000 for her.

It's hard to say what Joan's emotional state was at this point. Any nineteen-year-old would be worn down by constant interrogation and terrible living conditions. Joan was likely even more dispirited by not being permitted to attend church, make confession, or speak to a priest. While she remained stubbornly loyal to Charles, he was now doing the royal equivalent of refusing to acknowledge her because she was no longer one of the popular girls in school. She had taken an arrow to the neck, a sword wound to the thigh, and injury from her leap, none of which could be putting her in the most lucid state of mind.

She signed a confession to appease her French/English-sympathizing inquisitors, and from there had a lifetime of imprisonment to look forward to that likely included moldy food and water, diseased bedding, and attempting to avoid being raped by her jailors. Who knows what actually happened to make Joan "relapse" into cross-dressing (which was deemed perfectly acceptable by everyone until she became a liability), maybe her voices told her, "It's not going to get better from here, sister. Let's peace out." Maybe she had no other option. Maybe she wasn't really looking forward to twenty-ish years living like this. But she did put on men's clothing, which was her official crime, though she was accused of Witchcraft as well and was swiftly sent to the stake.

Lessons from Joan

If an illiterate, fifteen-year-old medieval farm girl without means or familial influence could make her way to the royal court and get an unlikely candidate crowned as king using only her natural glamour and the strength of her conviction, what Great Work couldn't you accomplish? Joan may not have had strong alliances with powerful women when she started her quest, but once her glamour helped her gain their support, she was unstoppable.

Empathy Is Not Optional in Glamour

When working with others, empathy is very important to accomplishing your Great Work, but it is not everything. You need both glamour *and* empathy to be an unstoppable force. Put simply, empathy is what you *do*, and glamour is what you *are*. In Hinduism, the god Shiva is *being* and the goddess Parvati is *doing*. If you are too much of *being,* while you may achieve enlightenment, you may also amble aimlessly through the cremation grounds smoking pot for an eternity. If you are too much of *doing,* you may get as much done as Martha Stewart but you may get caught up in laundry instead of enlightenment. Shiva and Parvati are married, symbolizing the unity of male (passive) energy and female (active) energy of the universe. When they are fused together, they form the deity Ardhanarishvara, who is both fierce and gentle as well as loving and destructive—all of the universe's possibilities in one balanced being.

Empathy is the starting place for the active part of glamour. Essentially, empathy is when you catch what someone else is feeling and you feel it yourself. For most people this is an automatic reaction. A loved one feels sad, so you feel sad in return. At this level, empathy is called *affective empathy.* If you can understand what someone is going through (loss of a parent, job loss, divorce, et cetera) because you've experienced it yourself, you are engaging in *experiential empathy. Cognitive empathy* is when you find how the other person feels about a situation by actively engaging with them through listening and asking questions. Finally, *imaginative empathy* is when you imagine yourself as the other person and figure out how you would react in their situation.

If empathy is not a skill that comes easily to you, don't despair. While it is important, it's not an exact science and has its own limitations. You won't always imagine how the other person is feeling correctly. Something that makes you feel angry if it happened to you may make the other person feel scared or sad. Empathy alone is unlikely to inspire you to help the other person. While you may feel happy, sad, or another emotion in that moment with the other party, you may then go about your day as you usually would without doing anything to help the other party. Even if you *don't* feel empathy for another person's situation, you may feel inclined to help her because you feel it's the right thing to do. There's also generally an unconscious human bias to want to help people we find adorable or attractive versus people who we don't find to be either.

You can utilize empathy and its limitations in pushing your revolution forward. First, let's work on our active listening skills. In the words of the immortal Judge Judy, God gave us two ears and one mouth for a reason. Do you talk a whole lot? Start by shutting up. This is infinitely harder than it sounds, as someone who often can't shut up.

Do you have trouble knowing what to say? You need to start asking questions and showing the other party that you are listening and not secretly a houseplant by actively engaging. If you don't know what to say, ask something like, "How did that make you feel?" Once a feeling that you can relate to is expressed, say something along the line of "I would feel the same way because of ... (whatever reason you would feel the same way)."

People Like People Who Listen and Water Is Also Wet

Not talking/actually talking is the first step here, but it gets more complex. You need to also treat the other party like she is the most important person on the planet. This is generally relatively easy when you like the other party but becomes significantly more difficult when you do not. Guess whose help you will more likely need in forwarding your Great Work? Correct.

Start this process by being completely present with the other party. Don't daydream and wander off in your mind while she's talking—find something interesting about what she's saying and ask questions to learn more or comment in ways that indicate that you are actively engaging. Checking your cellphone (unless you are expecting an actual emergency call/text) is the fastest way to say that you are checked out. It doesn't matter if the other person is, the other person is (probably) not plotting a tiny revolution … you are. At the same time, it's a delicate balance between interested and inquisitor.

As someone who tends more toward inquisitor than interested, I can understand the difficulty there. You aren't trying to shake a confession out of the other party (in most cases), you are attempting to build a genuine connection with them. A genuine connection is what's going to make the other party go the extra mile past making vague interested-in-you noises and into offering actual assistance with your Great Work.

This is where it is far more important to be a genuine human instead of trying to mimic a sociopath. After all of this heady talk about choosing your choice about your moral compass, this statement sounds suspiciously like me telling you what to do. Hear me out. You *can* of course choose to be a sociopath, but frankly you're not going to be very good at it. Can you generally tell when someone is really interested in what you are saying instead of just phoning it in? Can you usually tell when someone is genuinely passionate about something instead of putting on a show? Most other people can too, so it's not really a great approach. While you may have a more ambiguous moral compass, genuineness is a really important aspect of glamour.

Once Upon a Time

Let's consider some traditional faery lore as faeries as known for performing glamour magic. Many kinds of faeries, such as sluagh, pixies, redcaps, and their assorted dark-side-of-the-year brethren, don't really have a human sense of morality. They were spirits of the restless dead, inclined to drown passersby, and they painted their caps red with blood. They were also full of glamour, even with this mortally suspect sense of morality. Unseelie faeries could lure you to your death, keep you captive for days in Faerylands only to shove you back to the mortal world where ten years have passed, and exercise their power to make you do all kinds of things that you shouldn't be doing. But in most faery folklore, faeries couldn't tell lies.

It didn't matter if they were good (seelie) faeries (who were also plenty terrifying, especially if they felt slighted) or bad (unseelie) faeries. They could not lie. Oh, they could skirt the truth, they could change the subject until you forgot what you were asking, they could decline to answer your questions, they could get clever and phrase it as a riddle, but they couldn't lie. How could that much glamour work if it was tied to a complete falsehood? It couldn't, which is why faeries traditionally can't lie. There would be nothing for their magic to stick to if they could. There has to be that core of genuineness that comes from their inability to lie for their glamour magic to build off of.

If glamour is supposed to be about what is interesting and intriguing about you, how would a complicated web of lies (the first definition of glamour) help you achieve your Great Work? How could you truly build connections to other people if it's all a lie?

If you think about popular fictional examples of sociopaths, they always have someone who they have a genuine connection to: Hannibal Lecter to Clarice Starling, Sherlock Holmes to John Watson, time lords to their companions, and so on. What makes them glamorous in part to the reader is imagining that you could be that *one special person* that your sociopath has chosen to have a genuine relationship with, or conversely, that you would *have* that one special person whose life would essentially revolve around you. Even in those stories, having a genuine connection is an important aspect of the tale. Think about beneficial situations that have popped up over the course of your life. While a few of them may have arisen solely from luck, most of them have come from genuine connections you've formed with others.

You Need to Connect with People Who Hate Your Face

When dealing with enemies and frenemies, find genuine points to connect with. Finding common ground can make both yourself and the other person see each other differently, *especially* if most of your dislike for each other comes from the rumor mill and other people's opinions.

There are going to be times where you have to work with people who don't like you and/or whom you dislike, but remember our earlier discussion about Margaret Beaufort and Elizabeth Woodville, working together clandestinely to marry their children to start the Tudor reign. They founded a dynasty together and are well-documented in how much they hated each other's faces.

When you are making connections with people you cannot stand for whatever reason, finding some tiny piece of them that you *can* stand is the quickest way to a genuine, sincere connection. Maybe you both have Pomeranians, maybe you both are on Paleo diets, maybe you both like Danielle Steele novels, whatever. When you can start to actually care about this other person in some tiny sort of way, that's when it is more likely that they will care about your dog and pony show in return. If you can establish a surface connection, you may find it easier to establish deeper, sincere connections that start to take root between the two of you. Maybe you were the same age when you both lost your fathers, maybe you both have kids with special needs, or maybe you've both been through a divorce. Shared experiences and genuinely connecting about them together makes these roots begin to sprout green shoots. Maybe you'll find you were mistaken in your previous impression or maybe you will simply find yourself more tempered in your feelings. When you can open yourself to the experience without expectation (which is much easier said than done), new bonds can be formed.

At the same time, being completely naïve and believing that everyone is good all the time and no one has an agenda of their own will get you into trouble. Everyone has an agenda; you do, I do, your friends do, your parents do, your coworkers do, your lovers do, your enemies and frenemies do, your goddesses and spirits do, everyone. Sometimes it is in your best interest, sometimes it's what they believe is in your best interest, sometimes it is unabashedly not in your best interest at all. All of these outcomes are possible from all of the parties listed for different events that come along. No one acts one way all the time, including you. The more you can be aware of this and see what other people's agendas are and accept this about others, the more you will be able to have a clear view about others and be able to work with them.

Other people's agendas don't make them evil or toxic or any other exciting words per se, it just means they have a plan for their Great Work too, which you may or may not like and agree with. If you can see a place where your Great Work can fit together with their Great Work, you will be able to work together. It doesn't have to be the whole puzzle fitting together seamlessly, just one piece of yours and one pieces of theirs that can click into place together.

Remember details about the other party as best you can: what they get from Starbucks, the names of the people in their families, their interests, foods they can't stand, political beliefs, religious beliefs, music they like, as much as you can remember. If you are a diehard liberal and the other party is an extreme conservative, don't pretend to be conservative. The truth will come out in this social media heyday we're all having together. Instead, remember not to talk about politics. If the conversation turns political, gracefully change the subject to a more neutral topic that allows you to connect. Like most of the skills discussed in this book, this will take practice. You may want to deliberately put yourself in situations you know will make your blood boil (political conversations in the break room, disagreeable family members at dinner, Internet-based discussions) and figure out how you will either change the topic completely, or keep the conversation productive and neutral.

From a magical standpoint, when you make a genuine connection with the other party, you are forming a delicate bond between the collective energetic threads that reside in each of you. The more threads you can gently pull loose from the other person and tie to yours, the more likely they will be to help you achieve your Great Work. The more sincere this connection is, the stronger the tied threads are. This is why genuine connection is stressed over play-acting. From a Witchcraft standpoint, you will have a much stronger position if your energetic bond with the other party is robust. Glamour magic may not care about mimicry versus sincerity, but that won't suddenly make an insecure bond sturdy.

Most of Us Are Not Naturally Talented

People with a lot of natural glamour have an easy unconscious way of accomplishing this. We don't have that luxury, so it's going to be very awkward until you get better at forming these connections from practice. Think about people you know in your real life whom everyone automatically immediately likes. What do those people do that you do not do that you can work on? Again, concentrate on personal growth versus mimicry.

Jow is one of those completely annoying people whom 90 percent of the populace immediately loves and wants to befriend. He is so accustomed to being immediately showered with praise, affection, and adoration that if he meets anyone who dares to be part of that other 10 percent, he will instantly launch a one-person campaign for their fondness until they have fallen prey to his inherent easygoing glamour.

I am not one of those spoiled children of the universe. I have too many sharp edges, am too overtly motivated, and too clearly expect you to be as well; I seem standoffish, I talk too fast, I don't listen incredibly well, I tend to wool-gather or check my phone the second you cease to be interesting to me, I don't wear jeans or T-shirts, and if you meet me in person first and have not read my blog, I do not seem like someone who is very relatable. All of my Myers-Brigg ENFJ traits are immediately noticeable to new people who are less ambitious and promptly feel intimidated to whatever degree their internal world dictates and generally want to flee or not directly interact with me.

If they have similar ENFJ traits that are prominent, there will be sniffing and testing in a first meeting instead. Jow finds simply witnessing the sniffing and testing incredibly stressful and anxiety-producing, but I find it significantly less taxing than dealing with someone who clearly is afraid of me to some degree.

I couldn't be Jow even if I wanted to be; I will never smell like he does on an energetic level. I won't be easygoing, I won't be incredibly interested in your problems simply because you are vomiting them up in front of me; I am not invested in you immediately wanting to be my BFF.

I can, however, turn down the intensity and turn up my natural impishness, I can not be a jerk who punches out on other people and focus on the conversation at hand, I can consciously slow down my speech. These are all things I can do and have worked on for first impression purposes. What can you work on to make a better impression?

In learning to connect with other people, be sure to make mental notes about the other party. Can you tell when the other person is genuinely laughing? Can you tell when the other person is sincere? If the other party is naturally very glamorous, in many instances you will instinctively want to make their words and actions match up, even when they do not. Watch the other person carefully.

Does the way the other person perceive herself align with her actions? For example, does the other party think of herself as very charitable but you have never seen or heard of her volunteering or writing a check to charity? In most cases, it's not your place to correct how the person sees himself versus how he actually acts. He will likely continue to see himself as he had previously and see you as wrong for pointing out otherwise. This will in turn make him see you less favorably unless you are close friends, family, lovers, or allies and it's been already established that this kind of critique is welcome. It is far more important for you to mentally note these inaccuracies as they may come into play as you move pieces around the chess board to achieve your Great Work.

Multitasking Is Challenging Even for Prophets

In the Book of Judges and the Midrash, Deborah was your modern twelfth-century BCE career woman who juggled marriage and leadership over Israel as well as a demanding relationship with Yahweh as a prophet. In between these duties, she found time to discuss uprising tactics with the commander of her army, Barak, as the Canaanites had been busily oppressing Deborah's people for the last twenty years. During one of their rebellion study sessions, Deborah suggests to Barak that he should pull together ten thousand-ish soldiers to let loose the hounds of war on the Canaanites while she rides out to take care of the head of the Canaanite army, Sisera, and then there will be peace in Israel again.

There is a long pause while Barak gives Deborah the *girl, you are hella crazy* look and then tells Deborah that he would prefer if she came and helped round up the troops because convincing farmers to go to war and that they will actually come home is arduous work that is better suited to a judge. Deborah shrugs and basically says, "If that's what you want, loser. FYI, according to Yahweh, a woman is going to take Sisera's punk ass down, and you will always be remembered as a loser, loser." Always willing to let her underlings have a learning experience, she rides out to gather troops with Barak and launches a surprise attack on the Canaanites. The battle goes according to Deborah's prophecy, and the Canaanite army is completely destroyed.

Meanwhile, Sisera and Jael both independently see the writing on the wall that the tides would be turning. Jael was a Kenite, making her people neutral to both the Israelites and the Canaanites. Sisera sees his army getting slaughtered and hits the road, heading for the Kenite encampment. Jael is at home in her tent while her husband is out hunting, playing cards with the guys, or whatever men in 1100 BCE did during some unknown point in the day. Women were generally in charge of setting up the household, carting knickknacks from place to place, arranging the furniture, putting the tents up, and taking them down, so Jael is kicking back, putting Post-it notes on her IKEA catalog on how to better organize migrant living or whatever women did unsupervised during an undisclosed time of day.

Sisera comes rushing to Jael's tent and lets himself in, despite her husband not being home, and demands that she hide him from the Israelites. Also, how about a glass of water? Jael makes some casual flirty conversation to figure out what the hell is going on and learns that the Canaanites were just soundly trounced and the Israelites were looking for Sisera. While there is no way to know what Jael was considering while she popped open a bottle of milk and poured it into her best dish for Sisera, it was likely something along the lines of, "Well. I can hope that Heber gets his ass home before Sisera decides to be terrible, or I can make a command decision to curry favor with the new head Israelite chick in charge and take care of the problem myself."

All of the flirting and milk after losing a major battle has Sisera tuckered out. He starts yawning and rubbing his eyes like a sleepy toddler and Jael tucks him under a blanket and he falls asleep, feeling secure that since all of his demands have been met and then some, his important dude privilege will keep him safe and sound.

Jael finds her mallet and an extra stake in one of her bags and slithers over to where Sisera is sound asleep and drives the stake into his head so hard she nails him to the ground. Eventually, Deborah rolls into town with Barak and Jael is all, "Hey girl, I got something for you." Deborah mouths "I told you so, loser" to Barak. Deborah judges Israel until she dies forty years later, and Jael is given a place of honor both during her lifetime and in the Song of Deborah, which is one of the oldest pieces of song/ poetry to have survived.

Lessons from Deb and Jael

The lesson here is that you need to learn to be able to change as your situation changes, and you need to be able to make a very good educated guess as to what your opponents will do. Game theory is used in economics, politics, animal studies, and psychology among others to assess why a person or animal would make the decision they made in an interaction such as in actual game play, a social exchange, or dispute over resources.

In actual practice, rarely are two players evenly matched. It is unlikely that when you are dealing with other people to accomplish your Great Work that your intellect, size, appearance, success, strength, and income bracket are going to be exactly matched.

As we've discussed at length, you are likely the disadvantaged party in this particular interaction. The other party has something you want to assist you in accomplishing your Great Work, whether it's money, power, influence, prestige, or a really good discount at your favorite store.

A Game Theory Primer

What would be the payoff (benefit) for the other party to choose to assist you in your Great Work? Assessing motivation will assist you in deciding how to appeal to the other party for help. Will she like having a protégé, making your success a part of her success? Does he get a sense of satisfaction in knowing that he helped "fix" you? Does the other person value herself as being thought of as a charitable person? Have you helped him out of a jam and the assistance he will give you will render you both even in his eyes? Does she like to have others indebted to her? Does he like to be thought of as a martyr of kindness? Does she think that your success could be of use to her later if fortune's wheel suddenly turns against her?

You already know what your payoff from this exchange will be. In order to further entice the other party to aid you, it's important to understand what their payoff is too. You can use your glamour to subtly influence the other person if you can accurately gauge what his payoff will be. As previously stated, coming from a place of sincerity is what's going to get you somewhere. If your future success would be of interest to the other party, after making your petition to her, you could say something like, "It would mean so much to me to have you involved with this project. And who knows? If this goes the way I hope it will, I will be able to help you (because the discount at the shop got me an interview at a great company that's hiring in your field/because your sponsorship got this artistic project funded which gained media attention and I will mention your name everywhere/by getting you season tickets to the opera as a thank-you for introducing us)."

Very generally speaking, game theory dictates that people are divided into two groups: let's call them angels and demons. An angel will want there to be peace and fairness and would prefer to avoid violence to hold on to whatever is important to him. A demon will want whatever she wants, regardless of the wishes and well-being of others and will be willing to be aggressive to get what she wants and may use violence to get it. An angel may try to use reasoning with the demon to be non-violent and to respect her wishes, which may work. The demon may decide to take the angel's views into consideration to suit the demon's purposes, but the demon may not and instead may be willing to kill the angel for her own means.

As we have previously discussed, people are rarely so conveniently defined. Someone may be an angel in most aspects of life but be willing to use demon tactics in a few particular areas, and vice versa. Let's discuss an example. Rachel thinks it's wrong to steal but she is hungry and has no prospects for assistance to obtain food or money. Monica also thinks it's wrong to steal, and she owns a bakery. The laws in her town say that she must throw away all of her unsold food at the end of the day. Rachel doesn't want to steal, but she knows that she will soon starve to death if she doesn't eat. She could choose to ask Monica to give her leftover food at the end of the night, explaining she is starving and cannot get work (an angel strategy), she could ask Monica for a job in exchange for money or goods (an angel strategy), she could steal goods or money from Monica's shop (a demon strategy), or she could steal out of Monica's dumpster at the end of the night (a demon strategy). If any of these strategies work for her, Rachel's payoff is that she does not have to starve. Monica could be moved to give Rachel food or a job at the end of the night, which would give her the payoff that Monica feels she's a good person because she gave Rachel food or an opportunity. She could allow Rachel to steal from her, and the payoff for Monica would be to not feel guilty about putting Rachel in prison and not having to deal with closing the shop to go to court. She could disallow Rachel to steal from her by prosecuting Rachel in court, which would give Monica the payoff of setting an example in the community not to steal from her, ensuring her profit margin stays positive.

Rachel may choose which strategy she decides to use with Monica based on what she knows about Monica from her own experiences and the experiences of those she knows in the community. If she knows Monica to be charitable through her work in the community, she may ask Monica for a job or leftover food. If she knows Monica to not be charitable, she may take her chances and steal. If Monica is known for prosecuting thieves in her store, Rachel may decide not to steal from her and choose to steal from someone else. Rachel may also choose to employ what is known as a mixed strategy in which she is first an angel (Rachel asks for a job and

Monica gives it to her) and then a demon (even though Monica gave her a job, Rachel still steals from her anyway).

Game theory gives you an opportunity to logically look at a situation that may be helpful if the stakes are high or if your emotions are running hot about your current place in your Great Work. You won't know what the other party will chose ultimately and you likely won't know why they chose what they chose either, besides your speculation and the data you've acquired through your personal experiences and the experiences of others. However, if you can account for most of the probable outcomes and have a plan for each, it will help you to be more successful in your Great Work. Bear in mind, you are not omniscient. You will get taken by surprise by the other party when he does something you could not conceive of him doing. At that point, all you can do is try to make a decision based on the information you've previously gathered and the outcomes that you saw as possibilities and to attempt to turn up your glamour to recover as quickly as possible.

Should you look at every social interaction through these lenses? You *can*, that doesn't mean you *should*. If for no other reason than it sounds completely exhausting to go through all of this mental gymnastics simply to choose between *The Hills* and *Sex in the City* and pizza or Chinese takeout with a friend or a lover. However, when working toward your Great Work, game theory is one more weapon you have to use in conjunction with your glamour.

Optional Social Experiment No. 3

Objective: Learn to accept
assistance from others gracefully.

If you are someone who has trouble accepting help from others, you are going to have a lot of difficulty getting your battle started. Spend some time journaling about why you have difficulty accepting help from others, and then spend a day deliberately putting yourself in situations where you are forced to accept help from others, ideally a combination of strangers, acquaintances/coworkers, and loved ones. It does not have to be big asks from everyone. It can be as simple as accepting a literal door being opened for you. When you accept the help, look the other person in the eye, smile, and graciously say, "Thank you. I appreciate it."

FAILURE IS
ALWAYS AN
OPTION

Glamour likes to give the illusion that being fierce, owning the space that you stand in, giving an adorable little smile after saying something completely obscene and challenging, looking polished from head to toe and launching and completing your Great Work is effortless. Beyoncé's song "Flawless" became an instant meme because we would all like to think that one day, we will wake up as beautiful as Beyoncé with no effort required.

Beyoncé does not wake up looking like Beyoncé. Logically, we all know this. Emotionally, it's a different story altogether. It's easy to be dismissive of Queen Bey because she's at the top of her game. "Anyone can look amazing if they have a team of stylists, nutritionists, and personal trainers." True. But Sasha Fierce did not start out with a team of all of those things. She had to work her way up to that point, which meant there was a point in her early career where she had to put together an image for herself that eventually brought her to the current success. "Beyoncé has an amazing voice and is a really talented dancer." Also true! But natural talent is only going to get you so far without constant practice—just think about all the cautionary tales from *Behind the Music*.

Practice Makes Glamour

Most things in life that look completely effortless are the product of hours and hours of effort in honing a skill or talent. Most people can't do a perfect eyeliner cat's eye in the first attempt; the same can be said for jumps in figure skating, leading workshops, becoming published, starting a small business, becoming competent in parenting, and ironing a shirt correctly.

Our oppressors can buy organization. They can buy assistants to find documents that have gone missing in their offices, intricate closet systems to keep their clothes in perfect order, domestic help to hang the clothes that have fallen on the floor, personal chefs to make healthy dinners, personal trainers to keep their bodies toned, personal relations agents to keep their social media up to date and pristine, and staff to do all of the miscellaneous tasks that they no longer wish to complete in their daily lives.

We don't have these advantages. If we are lucky, we have friends, lovers, and family to help us not drown when we bite off more than we can chew for class projects, grocery shopping, and Great Work, for which we should always be incredibly grateful when graced with these advantages.

In not having access to these advantages that make being organized easier, it means we have two options: complain that we don't have the privilege, wealth, or opportunity that would make it easier and do nothing; or organize ourselves.

If you are going to use glamour as your weapon of choice in achieving your Great Work, you need to be able to use all of the aspects that we have been discussing that make up glamour together in a cohesive unit. Remember: beauty, charm, discipline, conviction, and organization. You are underprivileged. Your opposition has more power, more strength, more money, and likely more physical power. Is this a position where ignoring useful tools is helpful? As we've previously established, it is not.

The words "organization" and "beauty" tend to provoke the most emotionally resistant responses. You may have internalized feelings about not doing enough about either that are easy to wrap up in rhetoric. For example: "I don't know if I should wear lip gloss or not. I love how my lips look with it on but I hate the gendered expectation that goes with it and as a feminist, I feel conflicted about this."

In short, wrong. Is it wrong that you feel this way? As we are taught, feelings are never wrong. However, *actions* are often right or wrong. I am not personally invested in whether or not you wear lip gloss. I don't care. But you are wasting a lot of time and energy with the internal debate that you could be using instead to work on your Great Work. Decide to wear it because you value how you feel over the gendered expectation. Decide not to wear it because you value not feeling gendered over how it feels to wear lip gloss. Pick one, stick with it until it no longer feels right, and then re-evaluate.

Likewise with organization. You can tie that up with a lot of rigorous feminist debate about how you should not be obligated to live like Martha Stewart/your mother. That's fine. But if your Great Work is to start an Etsy shop that will support you financially and you don't have space to create crafts for your small business due to clutter, you have an issue. After a certain point, the time for feels has passed and the time for action is present. I will teach you a sacred phrase I tell myself when I am having an emotional response impeding me from action: *You don't have to like it, you just have to do it.*

Accomplishing Anything Great Is Hard

If you want to make real, terrifying headway on your Great Work, it's going to make you step outside your comfort zone and do things that make you desperately uncomfortable. If your Great Work was within your comfort level, you would be doing it already. You cannot tell yourself, *I want to win an ice dancing competition* and then content yourself with eating Doritos on the couch and watching ice dancing on television.

This is why your Great Work cannot be a whim—it must be something that you are willing to devote yourself to, something that you are willing to face heartbreak over, something you are willing to sacrifice for, and something that makes you face all of the things you do not want to face in order to get the thing you want most. Do you still feel confident about what you have chosen for your Great Work? If not, redo Esoteric

Experiment No. 1 and then come back here when you are very sure about the choices you've made for yourself.

Let's say you've decided that the goal of your Great Work is to change careers and become a hospice nurse. Don't worry if your goals are less lofty-sounding or more spiritually based; we are simply using this as an example to figure out how to make some real headway with this and becoming organized about it.

First, you need to select a nursing program that you want to get into and to determine if you have any of the credentials needed or if you need to start from the ground up. As you tour colleges, you will likely meet with advisors.

Organizational opportunity: Schedule time daily to research programs until you find three that suit your needs.

Glamour magic opportunity: Enchant a compass to sit on your desk next to your monitor as you are searching so that you find the right school, even if it's different from the three you picked.

Now you've found three programs that you like, so now you need to get into them.

Organizational opportunity: Be sure to fill out all required paperwork, have a friend edit your essay, and check with the schools to make sure they received your information.

Glamour magic opportunity: Be sure to meet with admissions and nursing school representatives, even if it's optional, as that gives you a face for these people determining your future. Choose your outfit carefully and be sure it projects the image you want. Use your glamoury to make a good impression by finding common ground to connect with these contacts. When you find common ground, use your glamour magic to give that connection an extra push to entwine your threads together. Follow up with these new connections with thank-you cards and casual friendly e-mails with relevant articles about your common ground that you found from reputable sources. Be open to unexpected options presented by these new friends such as a grant in an adjacent program.

Now that you've gotten into these programs, you need to do the Work and the work.

Organizational opportunity: Find out when is the best time for you to study with your current work schedule. Figure out how to maintain your household and family and what can be delegated. Make sure your selected parties whom you wish to delegate to are on board with it. Map out how long it will take to complete the program and figure out how to manage some internships at local hospitals on your winter and summer breaks for future job opportunities. Determine how much sleep you need, how much food you need to intake, how to manage some movement, and how to maintain self-care. If you fall behind, ask for help and move forward instead of wasting energy berating yourself. Maintain an excellent GPA.

Glamour magic opportunities: Meditate regularly on the position you want to step into and use your glamour to be able to recognize potential options. Use your glamour magic to keep current coworkers helpful and sympathetic by being charming to them and regularly baking goods that you put an intention toward keeping them sweet and helpful to you instead of trying to push you out when your performance lags due to midterms. Keeping up appearances is important for your work life and your position in the community; be sure to wear things that you have enchanted so other people cannot tell how tired you actually are so that they do not perceive you as weak (unless you want to be seen that way for additional assistance). Enlist professors and internship leadership to your cause so they write beautiful letters of recommendation for you for a future career in hospice.

You have now completed your nursing program and have started looking for a nursing position.

Organizational opportunities: Putting together a great résumé, following through after interviews with handwritten thank-you notes, keeping track of potential opportunities and networking opportunities in real life and online, curating the perfect outfit for interviews.

Glamour opportunities: Enchanting your job search so that you find the right position, even if it's different than expected, doing a regular glamour rite so others want to assist you in getting the right position, charming the interviewers so they have a great impression of you, enchanting an object you always have with you for interviews to get your choice of careers to select from.

I briefly laid this out as an example for you to understand both the practical and the glamour aspects to this. Your impulse will be to montage over the hard parts (it's what everyone does), especially once you've completed your Great Work. Let's go back to this example. You are going to school half-time, while going to work full-time. You probably have been out of school for some time and you may need to take some classes more than once. For you to become a registered nurse, it's going to take you about five years before you even are allowed to look for a new career. The job market is difficult in general, and lots of people want jobs in healthcare. It will likely take another six months to a year to find a job. During this time, your adult responsibilities don't magically fade away; your kids won't be suddenly autonomous, you don't get to quit your job, your home still needs maintaining, you need to maintain your support network and some sense of sanity. So, you are looking at six years of toil, *at least*. Six years of struggling to keep up with your studies and maintain your current career, six years of limited amounts of free time, six years of overwhelming responsibility.

Your Great Work is just that, great. If it were a minor work, you could probably achieve it in a few months. A Great Work is going to take a long time to accomplish. Once you have, much like childbirth, the hard parts will take on a gentle blur and you may even be nostalgic for them. But that doesn't mean that it was *actually* fun or easy.

I'm now nostalgic for when I was a nanny, but if I asked my mother about that time, she would likely recall how much my back hurt, how often I was sick, the stress over unpaid time off, my unwashed hair, my weight gain, when I would call her sobbing on the phone that I was never going to get anywhere as a writer or a creator and would never be able to have money saved for retirement, and nothing was ever going to work out ever; the future only holds darkness and dragons for me. Am *I* thinking about that when I miss being a nanny? Certainly not! I remember rocking them to sleep, hearing them say my name for the first time, the way their little faces would light up when they saw me, reading to them, playing kitchen, singing songs together, and hugging them so tightly.

Glamour Keeps You Motivated

It's completely normal to feel discouraged. Most people give up on their Great Work. That's why there are so many movies and books about people who almost made it or washed out. When planning your Great Work, you need to keep scale in mind. Maybe having a local but fiercely devoted fan base for your band is all you need to feel satisfied as an artist and you don't actually need a major record label deal, maybe you thought you wanted to make $75,000 a year but after some thought and research you realized $50,000 would be sufficient, maybe learning a new skill and becoming proficient in it is all you need and you don't need to be a leader in the field. Take a breath and figure out what you want.

At the same time, you shouldn't talk yourself out of dreaming big. Take an honest assessment of your skill set and what you've accomplished to date. Have people always admired you for what you're attempting to accomplish? Have you already had minor successes in your Great Work? You may simply be a late bloomer; many people work hard at their craft for a long time before becoming acknowledged. If this is something completely new, give yourself the opportunity to see if the new experience is a good fit for you. It may take longer to become proficient in your new skill set and it can be more of a challenge to learn new things as an adult, but that doesn't mean it's not possible.

Breaking your goals down into small steps with magical and daily-life work to do toward them empowers you to have small accomplishments along the way. If the goal is simply, "become a registered nurse" with no smaller steps, you are going to be more likely to give up because that is a very tall order to trudge toward for six years with no sense of accomplishment along the way. This is also likely to make you more inclined to want to abandon your Great Work and give up because you have grown weary of working so hard for no measurable treats.

You should make measurable treats for yourself along the way as each goal is accomplished. Small rewards for yourself—buying a novel, a good bottle of wine, a long bath, a pedicure, a new item of clothing, a night out doing something you want to do—as you accomplish smaller goals will help you keep yourself on track. As you accomplish your larger goals, larger rewards are in order, things like taking a class in something you have always wanted to learn, a new piece of technology for yourself, excellent seats for a concert, a massage, or whatever is special to you and would all help keep you motivated. You need to make sure there's a way to measure your progress so you don't lose focus.

Glamour in your everyday life will also help keep you from drowning. If your world shrinks down to nothing but drudgery, it makes you depressed and demotivated. It's hard to be happy and feel accomplished when you don't see any place to find joy in your life. Small pleasures will help you slog through incredibly long days. A nice home-cooked dinner arranged nicely, a bouquet of bright spring flowers, a brightly colored umbrella, a French *Vogue* at the bookstore with a cappuccino, and whatever restores your faith in beauty in this world can help you regain your perspective (and composure).

Sudden Success Can Cause Fear

Let us discuss success in your glamour, as there should be a noticeable change by this point. For some, it can be super exciting! Sudden flirtations, literal and figurative doors being opened, small favors, people now offering to assist you, new opportunities, all by virtue of how you've worked to wield your glamour. This could be giving you tremendous satisfaction in your power as a Witch as you incite your own personal civil war.

Alternatively, you may be considering locking your glamour down so tightly that your energy may as well be a princess in a tower with no door and a window forty feet up because this is super scary and intimidating for you.

If you are pleased with yourself, excellent. Continue to read this part in case you find yourself in a change of heart or in an unexpected situation so that you have recourse for yourself.

My frightened rabbits, you have likely noticed that now that you are lit up as brightly as a Christmas tree to the universe, you are getting a lot of attention you like and a lot of attention you don't. You may be feeling a bit awkward about being noticed much more than you previously had or you may even be overwhelmed by the attention. Part of this comes from being more accustomed to being the disempowered party in an interaction. If you are used to being overlooked and more familiar with playing the supporting cast in your life than being a protagonist, the transition can be a bit difficult. All those eyes on you, the new expectations that have been placed upon you due to your newfound glamour skills. It is not a fluid, effortless transition in most cases.

It would make our lives much easier if all we had to do was shake out our hair, wear what we were told is fashionable by our "betters," and take off our glasses. Now we are the most popular in school, like all the teen movies demonstrate. Those are the parts we remember anyway, because makeover montages are so fun. There's upbeat music, uncertainty about product use, and then *ta-da!*

But remember the parts that usually come after the montage where the protagonist is now forced to make some uncomfortable decisions: to feign stupidity or not, to date the less popular peer or not, to remain friends with the old friends or not, to harm less popular students or not. Even if you are past school age, you will be faced with new decisions that need to be made, much like our high school movie actresses. Transformation is difficult—the caterpillar becomes a butterfly but not before throwing all of her internal organs in a blender in the chrysalis first. You too will now need to make decisions for yourself that test your moral compass.

Your instinct may be to stop being so noticeable, to turn away from your glamour, to hide your physical form, to gain or lose weight to be less apparent to others, to hide your cleverness, all to self-sabotage yourself away from success. Maybe you feel you don't deserve this upswing in your life, maybe you feel afraid and overwhelmed, but whenever you want to hide, force yourself to confront what you want to hide from and make yourself not dim your glamour to make others more comfortable or to avoid attention.

The Best Defense Is a Good Offense

Everyone's impulse will be to tell you to better magically shield yourself, but in my experience, a stronger shield prevents the light of your glamour from shining as brightly as possible. You *want* to be noticed. That's why you're doing this. By your goddesses, by your spirits, by shopkeepers, by people in power, by people you want to seduce (or be seduced by), by your friends, by your family, by your coworkers, everyone. If you do what you've always done, you will get what you've always gotten. If you were pleased with your progress in your tiny rebellion previous to your glamour work and felt you were doing everything you could possibly be doing, you wouldn't be turning to Witchcraft and you *certainly* wouldn't be turning to glamour to achieve your Great Work.

You will have moments of doubt, insecurity, and uncertainty. In those moments, it's natural to even lapse into imposter syndrome where you feel like your achievements are based on other people's perceptions of you or luck and nothing to do with your Witchcraft or your hard practical work. You may feel like you don't deserve the success you've achieved because you used glamour to help yourself achieve it. You may feel that because these aspects are new to you, someone(s) will see the newness on your achievements on your glamour, magic, and success, and call you a charlatan.

In your day-to-day life, when these thoughts float up to the surface, the immediate solution is that you need to kill them with fire because they will only slow you down from achieving your Great Work. If you have a positive self-talk resistant brain, you can sternly tell yourself no when they come up. You could journal about your fears and the root causes, meditate to clear your mind of this broken thought process, mantra to let go of these thoughts, list your accomplishments to yourself, or do a regular rite where you cleanse yourself, or any combination of this general idea. But in the moment, when you are potentially getting called out by someone else or are performing in some manner publicly, you need a shot of magic to get yourself through it.

Esoteric Experiment No. 11

Objective: Call up your glamour when you feel anxious.

Choose a ritual space within your home. Wear clothing that makes you feel safe and comfortable: your favorite robe, your most comfortable pants, your lover's T-shirt. Encircle yourself with tiny mirrors that you purchased at your favorite craft store so that you are reflecting your intent all around you. As you lay down each mirror, say words of protection. Build a small temporary shrine to express your glamour within the circle, using items you find in your home and yard: fresh strawberries and cream, flowers from your garden, bread you have just baked, your favorite piece of jewelry, a sacred picture of your glamorous uncle, or beeswax tea lights. Gaze at your shrine and draw strength from the physical representation of your glamour you have built with your own two hands while being aware of its transient nature.

Relax. Lie down if you like. Become aware of your breathing until you are able to find trance space using whatever methods are most helpful to you. If you are not a visual person, think about your expedition in words, impressions, or whatever is most natural to you. Think about going inside yourself to your spirit's center, wherever that resides in you. This is your sacred space. What does it look like? What does it feel like? What does it smell like? What does it sound like? Take time to fully create this space within yourself.

Once you have created your space, start to explore it. As you explore, think about your glamour. Think about your glamour as a weapon, as a tool, as an instrument. In your space, find the physical representation of your glamour. You will know it when you find it; be patient and open to whatever it may be. When you find it, hold it in your hands and ask the object's spirit for its name. Call your glamour by name. Open your eyes.

When you find yourself in a situation where you feel doubt about your glamour and your power, mantra your glamour's name until you feel centered in your power again.

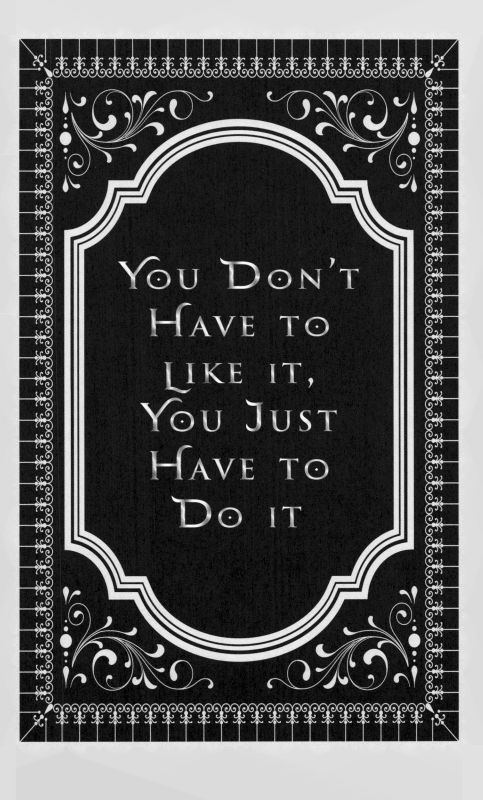

You may find that you sabotage yourself when you are close to achieving your Great Work. You dawdle on signing the contract, you put off doing the work others have commissioned to be done by you, you let yourself talk yourself out of going to important events or tell yourself other things are more important, you become afraid and stand on the edge of achieving your goals, too paralyzed to jump. For you to be able to accurately and effectively deal with self-sabotage, you have to have a really strong handle on when you are attempting to bullshit yourself and when you really need to take a moment.

Adhere to deadlines, have tracking information when mailing physical objects, do what you promised to do, figure out what your next small steps are for you to move forward, and make one small step that very day. If social anxiety and/or depression are hindering you from attending events that would be helpful in your Great Work, figure out what you need to push through it: Do you need to talk to your therapist about making a plan? Would having a friend attend the event with you make you feel safer? Would having a definite end time and exit strategy help you actually attend? Is a reward the following day an incentive to go? Does it help if you practice conversation with someone you trust about topics likely to come up? Does it help to have your fashion maven friend pick out your outfit and do your makeup? All of those things can be achieved—you just need to give yourself the time, space, and energy to achieve them. The more you practice anything, the better you will be at it. You may never be the best at it or even great at it, but you will definitely be better than you were when you started … and that's a prized accomplishment to be achieved.

Your actual physical body may rebel against your impending success with sudden stomach ailments, vertigo, colds, migraines, eczema, dandruff, rashes, acne, menstrual issues, and exhaustion. All of those manifestations are real and should be treated by a medical professional if previously un-experienced. Change is difficult and scary, and it causes very real stress on our psyches and our bodies because our minds, bodies, and spirits are con-nected. Don't be dismissive of your body's reaction to change, be sure to care for your body as gently and kindly as you would if a friend were experienc-ing these effects.

As if all of this discomfort wasn't enough, by now you have likely noticed that this extra attention does not exclude unwanted notice from creepers, overly zealous suitors, people who think soliloquy is conversa-tion, space invaders, and other vermin. Some of them will be strangers and therefore new to you, and some will be people you already knew who are now very interested in you.

Not Everyone Wishes You Well

Remember that your uprising is a small war, which means there's always an element of risk, danger, and harm to yourself and others. This sounds really scary until you remind yourself that whenever you step foot outside your house there's also an element of risk, danger, and harm. Sometimes you don't even need to leave your house!

When dealing with people who are undesirable to you for whatever reason, think first about if it will benefit you when your opponents show their hand about who they are, what they want from you, and if they could help you with your Great Work. As Maya Angelou said, "When someone shows you who they are, believe them the first time." This will require patience and some use of game theory. You need to be patient and strategic when attempting to get your opposition to reveal their plan to you and you need to maintain those aspects while considering what to do with that information.

Sometimes your opposition is simply people with opposing agendas and thought processes; they form the majority of your experience in dealing with the difficult. In those cases, you should spend some time considering how to better line up your agendas so that you can work together and figure out some common ground you have with these people so you don't spend all your time in a fit of loathing for them, as we've previously discussed. This will require compromise, which will require a lot of thoughtful consideration about what you are willing and definitely not willing to compromise. Ideally, you should be willing to compromise more than you aren't.

What if there is no reason for you to have to interact with some of these newly interested people who are causing you grief by demanding your time, energy, magic, and possibly even sexual favors? Should you simply accept this unwanted attention as the cost of glamour? You have been reading this volume faithfully, have you not? You are waging guerilla warfare—why would you accept an unwarranted attack on your person?

Shielding as hard as a tiny pill bug shows this adversary that they have power over you and could best you; it gives them the upper hand because it has allowed them the power to make you small and scared. You may *feel* small and scared but you must not *be* small and scared.

Let's talk magical assault first, before practical attacks. In this case, the best thing to do is counter-attack. Forcefully shove their oozy, slimy energy right back at them but mirrored to increase the effect. If you are very dexterous, you can use an actual mirror and an incantation of your choice to do this. If you are a bit more gawky, quickly figure out how you see/feel/sense/taste/perceive their energy. Then visualize (or whatever method you use for magic) increasing that energy as much as you possibly can, and then shove it as hard and fast as you can into their third eye/aura/root chakra/solar plexus chakra—whatever is most undefended, weak, and lazy. If you are unsure about where to shove their energy at them, no one likes to be hit in the face (third eye) or the junk (root chakra), so those are both good choices when in doubt.

Does that make you feel conflicted? As always, look to your moral compass for guidance. That said, Witchcraft does not require constantly turning the other cheek. You are defending yourself by attacking after having been attacked. You are demonstrating that you are not to be trifled with and will not lie down and take abuse.

Esoteric Experiment No. 12

Objective: Use when you feel
threatened but must hold your ground.

Concentrate on occupying the space you stand in. Shoot roots down into the earth and branches that spiral up to the stars through the crown of your precious head. Think about your breath and how it circulates cells through your body and how every time you take a breath, you are forming new life within you on a cellular level. Now think about yourself on an energetic level. You are afraid, so your energy is wound tightly around your body like a blanket. Keep breathing air into your energy that surrounds you to puff it up and make it bigger. Make yourself big and imposing—bigger than your opponent and much more fierce. Put your will into creating extra limbs, terrible claws, fierce tails, gaping maws with terrifying tongues, banshee blood cries, and wings that beat with fury. You are the embodiment of your goddesses' and spirits' most horrifying aspects. You are the Morrigan, Kali, Lilith, Hecate,

Nyx, and every primordial spirit that knows your name. You are not nice, you are not pretty, you are not accommodating. Your glamour is in your terrible fury and ability to eat all that oppose you whole. When the danger has passed, dispel this energy with a sharp exhale, as if you have blown out a candle, and look at yourself in a mirror to rearrange any bits that are out of place in your regular seeming from your Work.

Practice this skill at random times when you are not threatened at all or only slightly threatened. If you are friends with other Witches, work together on improving this skill. Observe how you change, observe the change in others around you. Use this as your magical self-defense.

You Shouldn't Make Everyone Happy

Magic is a good option to have and you should utilize it, but you will want to have some mundane applications as well. In previous chapters, we discussed the importance of being able to read others. This is especially important when you find yourself in a situation you don't want to be in: trapped behind a table at a bake sale, trapped on a bus or plane, trapped at a party where someone else drove—any number of situations where it can be difficult to escape. Start by listening to your intuition. Is your gut telling you that this person has bad intentions toward you? Do you feel unsafe? Do you not trust the other person? It's easy to want to dismiss these feelings, especially if you have been socialized in a feminine sort of way, regardless of your gender identity, because you have been trained to please others.

You know what won't please that person? Abruptly excusing yourself, asking the flight attendant for another seat, standing up to make a pretend phone call, or forcibly calling the other person out for making you feel uncomfortable. You have been socialized in a feminine manner. The undesirable person in question will consciously or unconsciously use that to their advantage and remind you that it is your job to make them feel liked, regardless of your personal feelings.

For some of us, it actually *is* our job to make this person happy, especially in sex work fields, administration fields, care fields, and customer service fields. Because of this, we will sometimes obediently perform whatever task the other party feels entitled to either because of our socialization or because it is literally our job. Sometimes we will silently accept the harassment because we are afraid to call attention to the fact that it's unwanted for fear of repercussion that could end in job loss or physical, emotional, or sexual assault.

We have been taught that the validation given by others is critical to our sense of self so even though we are filled with loathing for this undesirable person, we still somehow want this other person to think that we are nice and likeable. If this undesirable person thinks we are nice, accommodating, and likeable, it means we're a good person because the undesirable person said so. So we agree to stay, even when we shouldn't. We have been indoctrinated to not make a scene, to go quietly and not cause a fuss. As Witches, as people wielding arcane power and using glamour as a force, we don't need to be thought of as nice. Powerful, fascinating, noticeable, yes. Nice and accommodating, no. When you start to accommodate due to your socialized conditioning, consider if that's the action you actually want to take. Sometimes it benefits us and sometimes it doesn't.

But we need to stop going along to get along; we need to stop doing that right now. If you want a real revolt, you need to be willing to cause a commotion, even if it's only in your head as you are going against your socialized training.

You need to figure out what the best ways are for you to deal with these situations head-on without putting yourself in danger. Sometimes walking away and making up an excuse works, sometimes it will be a flat and completely disinterested monotone saying, "No, I don't want to do that," sometimes making a breezy joke helps ("Oh honey, you couldn't handle me, bless your little heart"), sometimes looking your undesirable person dead in the eye and saying, "You have no right to say that to me. The only one who has agency over my thoughts, feelings, and actions is me, and if you try pulling this shit again, you will be very, very sorry."

It's critical to learn what response is warranted when and what will keep you out of harm's way at the hand of this undesirable person. You need to be willing to learn how to escape uncomfortable situations unscathed. We have been trained to disregard our internal sense of danger. Never, ever do that. If you start getting a bad feeling about a person or a situation, get out. Immediately. Using whatever means necessary. It may have been unwarranted, you may feel foolish about it. But it's much better to wonder if someone was really a nice person with good intentions deep down inside than to have proof that they were not. Use the exit strategies we talked about in conversation. Put some physical distance between yourself and the undesirable person. If they try to get into your space, continue putting space in between the two of you. If they try to make you feel guilty or stupid for putting space between the two of you, you were obviously correct about that person. Tell the undesirable person that you are not comfortable being that close together. Put a physical object between you and the undesirable person. I feel safe with my shop at public events because there's always a table between myself and my clients unless I choose otherwise. In my setup, it is physically impossible without crawling under my table to get past that barrier. Have a signal with a friend or lover that they know means you need their help to escape immediately. Screaming and self-defense are also always options we have. Don't be afraid to use Esoteric Experiment No. 12 with great impunity in these situations.

Let's say you could either walk to work, which will take more time and energy, or be trapped on a bus with the same terrible undesirable person every day; you may prefer to walk. However if your work ends after dark and your workplace location has a high occurrence of crime, you may prefer an enclosed space with many witnesses. You need to be able to plan for known potential dangers, be quick on your feet about unknown peril, and be forgiving of yourself when you are flustered. Consistent time, energy, and attention to honing yourself to be better prepared for the unknown will make you less flustered.

If you've been in situations where you were powerless, it's never your fault. Please know that. Cunning, calling for help, training in self-defense, and doing all of the "right things" you were taught sometimes is not enough. Someone who wants to cause harm will cause harm. We are trying to learn how to shift the deck, but sometimes it's not enough. If you've been assaulted, therapy can help to work through that. You are owed whatever justice and vengeance you feel you need to help yourself, through our legal system and magically if desire. Even in "lesser" circumstances, where someone made you feel uncomfortable or obligated toward them but did not assault you, if you could not figure a way out of the situation and instead stayed silent to avoid escalating the situation, you survived to fight another fight, which is sometimes all we have.

But we cannot let our previous experiences beat us into submission. Glamour demands your right to take up space; glamour demands your right to present yourself the way you want to be seen by the world; glamour demands your right to shine brightly; glamour takes a steel spine, courage, and cunning. Taking up space when we've been taught to apologize, speak softly, and not be noticed is terrifying. Suddenly, you are an object for your oppressors' gaze where you are now required to perform like a lap dog for their amusement. *You're so pretty when you smile! Come over here and talk to me! Give me a kiss! Won't you sing for us?* It can be difficult in the moment to know what to do when it happens. You can consciously choose to perform for your oppressor, like Jael chose, as you bide your time to figure out how to drive the allegorical stake through your oppressor's brain. You can politely refuse. You can scream your rejection. You can say something clever and escape.

The difficult heart of the question is, "Is this a person you may need later for your Great Work?" If you write a scathing report on your blog or call HR on her, your oppressor is not going to want to help you. Many times, it is very much worth burning that bridge, salting the earth, and finding another way. You don't have to sell out your conscience to achieve your Great Work; you are not obligated to accept your oppressor's snail trail all over your hands. Sometimes, however, it is worth biting your tongue and finding a way to twist your oppressor's hand to your advantage. You need to take some time and weigh your options carefully. Only you will know what is an acceptable situation for your moral compass and what is not. This is not a path of Good Girls/Bad Girls—this is a rebellion with a lot of shades of gray. Mistakes will be made, grace and gentleness can be given to ourselves. No one leads an insurgence unscathed.

Your Bestest Frenemy

We've dealt with the more obvious people who are going to be difficult to interact with, so now let's get a little closer. Most of us have at least one person in our lives we love to hate, that we both love and distrust, that we can't stop ourselves from competing against in a never-ending *Jennifer's Body* Jennifer Check vs. Needy Lesnicki–type escalating struggle. Frenemy. For most of us, with age, we can mostly outgrow this relationship but will still find ourselves falling into this seductive, familiar pattern until we recognize the other person for who they are.

We try to tell ourselves comfortable lies about why we've allowed ourselves to be in this situation: the frenemy has a long history with you so he gets you, you've both had some good times together, competition can inspire you to be your best self.

Right.

There are a few relevant points that you need to keep in mind as well: Your blood pressure is likely higher when interacting with a frenemy than with an outright opponent/oppressor. A long history doesn't magically create a healthy environment; if it did, everyone's family dynamic would be amazing. Competition stops being productive when you stop using that energy to become better, faster, stronger, and instead use that time to lie on the floor whining to your besties about your frenemy, which is likely what you are doing. You've probably fought with your actual friends and they likely have habits you find irritating. Are you constantly talking about past fights that have been resolved and obsessing over their peccadillos? No.

Why do you choose to stay in this situation? Humans generally *love* things that are bad for them. The forbidden has always been delicious. You *know* what you're supposed to do in most cases: put some distance between the two of you, stop engaging, and focus on your Great Work. Are you doing this? Probably not.

It's so addictive, that rush of triumph when you feel you've bested your frenemy verbally, in achievement, or in physical presentation. It's a scrumptious high that's hard for even the most self-disciplined to resist. However, once you've crowed your triumph to your besties, you're right back to the beginning of the cycle where you are trying to figure out how to next best your frenemy.

We've agreed that glamour should be used to achieve your Great Work and that going to war to achieve a Great Work is often necessary and can put us in unknown and often fraught positions. It could get dirty. It could get messy. Should you use glamour to go to war against your frenemies? As always, you are in charge of your decisions and the consequences that follow them. You are free to do what you choose.

Let's step aside from your frenemy for a moment and use a hypothetical example that most of us won't encounter in our lives to demonstrate glamour-based decision-making and consequences. Since it will be out of most of our everyday life experience, it will be easy to look at the methodology without getting caught up in extenuating circumstances and excuses you doubtlessly have about your frenemy. *Should you use glamour to acquire black tar heroin?* You could. You could use your glamour to become friends with people who use, who will then introduce you to their dealer. You could then use your glamour so the dealer becomes enamored with you and then allows you live with her and have all the heroin you want. Is a crippling addiction, possibly being turned out to become a dealer yourself, and potentially dying of an overdose a well-thought-out and executed Great Work? By most people's moral compasses, it is not. Just because you *can* do something, doesn't mean you *should*.

Bringing it back to your bestest frenemy, the root of the issue when going to war with them is that you are unlikely to ever conclude your business with your frenemy to a level that you consider to be sufficient quid quo pro for the injustices you received at their hand. Instead, you are far more likely to get caught up in an ever-escalating revenge cycle a la *Kill Bill, Hamlet,* and *Xena: Warrior Princess* or any soap opera (and most actual operas). Is that what you chose for your Great Work, back at the beginning? Did you open your heart and spirit to your true self, to your goddesses and spirits and what came to you is, *I will overthrow frenemy?* I suspect not. Since it was not your established Great Work, it is simply a distraction. So in just about every circumstance, you should not invest that level of time, energy, and magic in going to war with your frenemy. Again, just because you can, doesn't mean you should.

If you would like to actually step away from this cycle, you need to first acknowledge that you are an equal player in this arch-frenemyship. It would not have escalated to whatever point it has escalated to without a healthy dose of you also hating frenemy's face back. You've both taken the time and care to build epic spite shrines to each other in your respective heads. You are also engaging in backhanded compliments to take the other person down a peg ("Your stocky build really helps you pull off those boots!"), you are never admitting failure publically or to frenemy so they will never get the advantage over you, you are pretending with them that your one-person PR campaign on social media is your actual life instead of your projected life, and you are possibly actively sabotaging your frenemy.

Your enemies and oppressors are worth this level of attention, possibly. Someone who gets under your skin because they have something (possibly just an infinitesimal amount more than you) that you do not have is not worth this level of attention.

It's time to have some real talk with yourself about what you want that your frenemy has and to make concrete plans about how you can achieve it for yourself instead of constantly word-vomiting about frenemy like the rest of the world is your reality television show confessor. Get on your grind, do your Great Work, create some glamour, and stop being stalkeresque.

Unfollow their social media quietly. Be genuine when you interact, which will build more actual glamour than this fake dog and pony show you've been participating in. Don't escalate, don't try to one-up—it actually gives you a weaker position as it shows your insecurity. If you start to become heated and involved in your two-person *telenovela* where obviously whatever annoying behavior done/thing said is completely about you, because everything is about you (just like everything is about frenemy), take a breath and assign a neutral reason for whatever made you irritated.

As discussed, you could of course use glamour to attempt to control another person such as your frenemy. Doing so, however, requires constant care and vigilance, which is more work than it's worth.

No matter how strategic you are in attempting to control another person magically, you will not be able to account for every possible outcome that comes from it and may not enjoy the end result. Finally, when you are working on another person, you are tying yourself closer to the other party. Sometimes that will be a worthwhile consequence, but often it will not be as it tends to make you obsessive and overly invested in the other party's life which doesn't do anything too fantastic for you. So while as always you are welcome to do what you want magically as I am not here to teach you how to behave, but I am also not here to teach you how to get yourself out of a mess either.

Let us focus on using our glamour in a way that will be much less tedious and Sisyphus-like by focusing on what's significantly easier to control and manage: our own actions. If you are genuinely stepping back (and not simply telling yourself that you are), your frenemy may not be ready yet to give up this intimate relationship the two of you have taken so much time and energy to build together. It is very likely that she will ramp up everything that makes you want to go to war. If you choose to actively engage, you just restart the cycle.

Don't take the bait. The bait is *designed* for you to want to take it. It's meant to be delicious. It's meant to catch your interest. It will also be constructed to hide the hook that will pierce your tender mouth and pull you out of the environment you need to survive. It is critical that you ignore the bait, no matter how much you desperately want to take it.

Instead, choose a new path. Intentionally choose minor flaws and failures to showcase to your frenemy. It will force your frenemy to see you as an actual fellow human instead of a social media campaign. Steer the conversation so you can give actual, heartfelt praise for your frenemy, which will de-escalate the situation.

Security Comes with Practice

You have come to a place where you have developed your glamour into a full weapon that you are *choosing* not to use against this person. Instead, focus on watching your physical tells that display insecurity: nail biting, petting your own hair, touching your face, talking too fast, chewing on anything that is not food (pens, your lips, headphone cables, whatever), too much smiling (it makes you look like a beauty pageant contestant and not in a good way), twitching your fingers, jiggling your leg, cracking your knuckles, too much head tilting (as it bares your neck, which can be seen as a submissive gesture), condensing your body as though you are afraid to take up the space you actually embody, and playing with your jewelry or clothes. If you are flirting, much of this can be construed as quirky and cute. You aren't flirting here, you are sending the message that you will not engage and you are confident in your power. Wiping these tells from your physical vocabulary will also assist you when dealing with actual enemies and oppressors.

Think about it this way: Do you ever see political candidates who are vying to become president of the United States showing nervous tells when giving speeches? Do you ever see celebrities or royals showing nervous tells during televised interviews? No, you do not. You need to have your body language on point, not simply when dealing with frenemies, but in critical battles that impact your Great Work where you may be called to speak during a conference, a meeting, or even more publicly. Video yourself having conversations with people (with their permission) while working to not use any of these tells, and then watch yourself to see how successful you were.

Esoteric Experiment No. 13

Objective: Cut the ties that bind you to a frenemy.

Wear clothing that makes you feel confident or choose to be nude. This rite should be completed in your bedroom at twilight. You will need scarlet thread and scissors. The thread material is your choice: nylon, cotton, silk, or whatever you find at the bottom of your sister's sewing box. Embroidery scissors will be the easiest for this. Close the door and then seal the space shut by rubbing aloe vera from an aloe frond around the frame of the door while saying words of protection. Seal any windows, additional doors, and mirrors the same way. Sit on your bed and make a circle around yourself out of stones of your choosing—polished river stones, washed rocks from your yard, rough amethyst points, whatever works for you. Draw up energy through yourself using whatever method is best for you. As you start weaving the thread around your non-dominant hand, say out loud anything that you've said or done to your frienemy that makes you feel bad, not what you think you should feel remorse for but what you actually feel bad about. It may take some time, but be patient with yourself. When you have named everything out loud, look at your hand and the way the thread looks and feels around it. Sit with that for a moment. Resolve to not be tangled up in these behaviors any longer. Contemplate what you will do to no longer behave in that way. Then grant yourself grace and pardon for your previous actions and seal your intention within yourself to act in a way that you find favorable. Cut the threads that bound your hand from working to assist you to behave the way that you want to behave. Wash your hands with warm water, salt, and lemon to be done with allowing yourself to get caught up.

Hate Isn't the Opposite of Love, Indifference Is

Let us move on to the even trickier part of your glamour. Now that you are more polished, more poised, and intent on revolution, it won't only be enemies, random people, and frenemies trying to take you down—it's also going to be your nearest and dearest. Before we start on how your loved ones are going to try to put you back in your place, it's important to take a breath and remember that they are your *loved* ones: people you love and people who love you.

When you are down and feel like you will never accomplish anything and that you will wash out before you even make it, they are the people who will bring you back up. They will take on extra work to make sure you have enough time for your Great Work; they will listen to your frustrations, wipe your tears, cheer you on, accept your lengthy absences and long texting pauses with grace, go to your first shows/readings/whatever, and tell you that what you do is important and has meaning.

Granted, they will be more inclined to do all of these things if you communicate openly and honestly, and they will be more helpful if you make sure they're on board for these dramatic changes you are now planning to make as it will affect their lives too (*I know this is going to be really hard while I work twelve-hour days and we do craft shows on the weekends, but we'll be able to go to Europe like we always dreamt of with this money. Are you willing to do the majority of the housework and pour all the candles to make this happen?*).

It is really difficult to enact sweeping life change without the support of your loved ones. So remember that their lives are harder during this time too, and showing them that you appreciate everything they are doing to help you in the name of achieving *your* dreams will help everyone get along better while you figure out your Great Work.

As we have previously discussed at length, glamour is subtle and tricky and works on many different levels. It is completely possible (and likely) for your loved ones to feel proud of your accomplishments while also feeling resentful as hell about what they have sacrificed for you to get them. Your loved ones may also feel jealous of the attention you are receiving from others, they may feel insecure that they could be left behind, they may feel they are working just as hard as you but have less to show for it, they may feel less accomplished than you when they previously felt you were less accomplished than them, and they may envy the opportunities you are now being presented with.

The Evil Eye Is for Everyone

The *malocchio* (the Evil Eye) doesn't need to be wielded by someone with any magical experience; it doesn't even need to be intentionally wielded at all. Your loved ones may not realize on a conscious level that they are having all of these feelings about your recent successes. Love has always been a complicated emotion and is rarely untouched by darker emotions. Modern teenaged girls are excellent examples of this. Jacob Clifton wrote fantastically about *Gossip Girl* and summarizes the complexity of Blair and Serena's relationship thus: "It's about two girls that love each other so much, they have to hold tight to each other, no matter how many times the one gets screwed over and the other is rewarded for no reason. And this is riveting, because you are always one or the other."

The same is often true in actual life, and if you were once perceived by those closest to you as the one who was usually screwed over but now is rewarded for (in their mind) no reason, that will cause friction. Change causes friction in general, but you rising above your perceived station is going to be poorly received by the ones who love you most because now they are forced to consciously or subconsciously question their choices and their decisions they've made about their lives.

This may result in less sympathy for when life is difficult for you (or a vampiric amount of interest), more trash-talking behind your back than usual (likely about how you now think you are better than everyone else), and conscious or unconscious machinations to put you back in your place—or better, lower than you were when you started.

As much as humans love a success story, they love a morality tale where you overreached and were smacked down because of it and now have no chance of ever rising up again. Now you are meeker, less beautiful, less desirable, less successful, and more conscious of your place and your betters.

It's enough to make any sensible person not want to get out of bed ever again if this is what people you love are going to do to you, let alone what your despots and undesirables will attempt on top of it. For most sane, rational, loving people in your life, they won't *mean* to (your frenemies will be a different story). It won't make it hurt any less or lessen the damage but remember you too are not immune from the sickening thrill of *schadenfreude*. You are not St. Teresa of the Little Flowers; you too occasionally will indulge in this guilty pleasure.

Try to be gentle with the people who actually love you (and whom you love back). Remember that for most people, change is one of the scariest things that can happen in life. It makes people's lizard brains go ballistic. While our intellectual brains will understand that there is an implied negative to the phrase, *if you do what you've always done, you will get what you've always gotten*, your lizard brain sees this as a positive. If you get what you've always gotten, then you know what to expect! There's less danger and less failure! You will likely not die that way! Not-death is the goal! Except, if you are safe and comfortable at all times, it's very difficult to accomplish an uprising.

Most people in your life want the comfort of routine and the pleasant predictability that Facebook, Candy Crush, working a nine-to-five job, being in a long-term relationship, watching television, and a little bit of comfort eating/drinking/smoking has to offer. It's important to remember that choosing that is a choice, just like choosing to incite mini-insurrections is a choice too.

When someone shoots the Evil Eye at you, you will likely feel it or notice it in some way. When you do, yank it out of you as quickly as possible. Whether or not you want to shove it right back into them is up to you. Generally, in my personal experience, I feel it like a dart in between my shoulder blades where my bra band sits, at the back of my heart chakra. When I pull it out, I literally make a yanking motion to get it out of me. It physically hurts me when I do this, but I can't go about my business with a dart sticking out of my back. I then use Reiki on the spot afterward.

Wearing a hamsa draped over this part of your body may help as well to keep yourself from taking too much of the Evil Eye.

While you likely shouldn't work much on people you love because it tends to get twisted up and convoluted eventually (and it's exhausting for you, as previously mentioned), there's no reason why you should be afraid to sweeten their disposition toward you with some honey and cinnamon-infused baked goods … and cloves too if you suspect gossip. When you are mixing your baked goods, focus on all of the positive feelings you have toward the people you love and all of the positive feelings you want them to have toward you.

Here is where it is very exciting to imagine oneself as important enough for someone else to be actively working on you. It alleviates the need to take personal responsibility when everything doesn't go to plan, it means you are so important that the other person has built a spite shrine to you in their heads. Sadly, it is very unlikely that any of us are that important to spend so much time and energy on hexing.

However, if enough people are throwing little tiny Evil Eyelets at you, it eventually will make you feel like garbage. You will feel tired, drained, lethargic, disinterested in things you are usually interested in. Obviously, here is a good place to check to make sure you are not suffering from depression or coming down with the flu. If you aren't shielding harder and no one is specifically working against you, how do you fix this? You need to look at your internal energetic fish tank. Do you have suckerfish or a snail cleaning off the gunk that you are acquiring by dealing with the outside world? If you don't like fish, how about some mice, spiders, goats, or crows? Pick a creature of your choosing that is good at chewing through things, cleaning things, and digesting the indigestible.

Esoteric Experiment No. 14

Objective: Regularly cleanse
yourself of others' ill wishes.

*Find a representation of your creature. Fur mice for mice, for
example. Live creatures aren't the best idea because they have
a naturally short lifespan. Create a very small-scale version of
their habitat: a tiny fish bowl for your suckerfish with black
gravel and a jaunty little treasure chest, a shoebox diorama
that you create. Learn what your creature would like as a treat
and obtain it. Your kitchen is a good location for this rite, as
you are creating spirits. Hold the representation of your creature in your hands, draw up your glamour, and breathe into
the representation until you feel the symbolic creature stir with
life. Be patient, as this may take some time. Once you do, offer
your new spiritual companion the treat you selected. Ask your
spirit if they would be willing to clean the negative energy off
of you in exchange for offerings like these on a weekly basis. If
your spirit doesn't agree, thank them for their time and try a
different kind of creature. Remember, you are making a pact
with a spirit. If you don't honor your part, they will likely act
out against you. If for any reason you think that you no longer
need this arrangement, thank your spirits for their hard work
and release them from the pact as you release yourself.*

Failure Isn't Always a Breakthrough

We always like to annotate failure. We are failing better, we haven't failed
yet per se, we just haven't succeeded, we used our failure as an a-ha! moment and now we are all media moguls. The desire to obfuscate failure is
understandable. Who wants to sound like a sad, whiny Coldplay song?
For most people, failure feels bad, especially if there are critics who are

eager to tell us if we had simply done x or y, we would never would have failed in the first place. We are expected to have learned from our mistakes as clearly and simply as the morality tale about the scorpion and the frog teaches us. What if sometimes you're the scorpion and sometimes you're the frog and you don't always know which party you are?

Getting back to our historical riot grrls, let's look at a really terrible example of failure. The kind that's so bad that you can't come back from it and you've lost everything you ever had to fortune's wheel.

More of a Wolverine Than a She-Wolf

Queen Margaret of Anjou was not born and bred to be a she-wolf as many (white dudebro) historians like to paint her. She probably wasn't actually a vicious beast of war at all. This is important to note because history has no problem othering Queen Margaret. While mitigating factors are often presented about Richard III (who likely played a part in the murder of the two child princes, if you recall) and Edward IV (who may have been Queen Elizabeth Woodville's husband, but still dragged men out of church sanctuary and had them killed on church grounds), Queen Margaret is still portrayed as an even less sympathetic version of Lady Macbeth. In many current historical versions, she *still*—hundreds and hundreds of years later—does not get to be a person. No mitigating factors are given, no wrenching tales are told about how she had it hard, too. She was just a bitch who overreached, to this day. If royal blood couldn't protect her from being called an overreaching bitch, you can rest assured that it is highly likely while working to achieve your Great Work, you will be called the same if not worse.

In reality, she was likely received by the English reasonably neutrally, but she was going to have a difficult time of it to begin with as a French-woman whose only friend was the Duke of Suffolk, who had just been soundly trounced by Joan of Arc and the French, making him voted Least Popular by the other lords.

Queen Margaret wasn't able to win over the generous populace in her early days. While she was clever, witty, and very beautiful, she was also very conscious of her position and almost immediately had her new husband, Henry VI, hand over portions of France that were held by the English back to France, which was never going to be something the general English population was going to like.

In her early days, she was more concerned with how her household was running and matchmaking within it than making a splash in the political arena. Despite being in her late teens, she kept her attention on everything and wrote letters with very specific instructions on her wishes for the many households and estates she ran. It is likely that she had a much larger allowance than other royal ladies in her age group. Queen Margaret wasn't messing around with her allowance like the other royal ladies who spent theirs on clothing, jewels, and lapdogs. Instead, she used it to purchase gifts and influence potential allies, even in her early days of rulership, which is a pretty badass use of one's allowance at nineteen.

Her lack of popularity was also due to the king himself. He was mentally ill (likely, schizophrenia) and made plenty of unpopular decisions on his own, including courting the friendship of France (whom we've established we hate). He could not keep his nobles from constantly fighting amongst each other and was known to be capricious in his punishments. The king was an anointed royal of England and thus most of the population was disinclined to criticize him because that would be like criticizing God's wishes, which left Queen Margaret, as a Frenchwoman, a suitable proxy.

As Henry was prone to catatonic states, that left Queen Margaret to make the decisions, something the women in her family were known for—her grandmother, Yolande of Aragon, and her mother, Isabelle of Lorraine, ruled in the absence of husbands or sons. This was every bit as popular with the dudebro lords as you would expect it to be, which kicked off the War of the Roses.

She directed various battles, sometimes from Scotland and eventually from France as well. Blame for the brutal sacking of Ludlow, which included arson, rape, and theft, is still laid at her feet. This conveniently ignores the sacking of other battlefield towns that the other would-be kings committed. She is an unrepentant she-wolf but boys will be boys, right?

In her own medieval glamour play, Queen Margaret was not above befriending former bitter rivals who had turned against King Edward, such as his own brother, George, and the Earl of Warwick. She immediately betrothed her son to the Earl of Warwick's daughter, Anne. At this point, Queen Margaret is in France, figuring out a way to land in England and reclaim the throne for her husband and then her son. She arranges for an army comprised of mercenaries and Lancastrians and plans carefully with the Earl of Warwick about how to end the civil wars and regain her rightful throne.

The wars end here not just because of the alliance forged between Lady Margaret Beaufort and Queen Elizabeth Woodville (who went on to found the Tudor dynasty), but because Queen Margaret's son is killed in battle. Her husband, the other king, dies in captivity a few weeks later in the Tower of London (likely murdered).

Queen Margaret, once so unstoppable, once so ferocious, so determined to keep her family's legacy no matter what it cost, is completely broken. Her legacy is gone; she has failed. She spends the rest of her life in shabby gentility in France. Once, she was the French terror that constantly threatened England but now she is simply…forgotten.

Lessons from Marge A.

While Queen Margaret should likely be remembered much as Lady Margaret Beaufort is remembered, as a patroness of education, she is remembered not for founding Queen's College in Cambridge, but for her bitter defeat and ruin. She is a cautionary tale for what happens when a Bad Girl overreaches. Sometimes, we are the Moirai's darlings for only a short while and then ground under their feet with no way to recover ourselves. Some failures can't be recovered from. Do you dare to risk ruin for your Great Work?

There Are Many Reasons for Failure

In Amy C. Edmonson's article "Strategies for Learning from Failure" in the *Harvard Business Review*, she discusses failure as a spectrum of personal accountability, which is critical because blame plays such a large role in failure. Once you can be assigned blame, you are also typically assigned guilt, anger, and sadness to go with it. Everyone wants to point their finger at someone else, as it absolves them of responsibility. But when absolving oneself of responsibility, you are also absolving yourself of opportunities for growth and reassessing the situation. While as a culture we like to use fitspiration phrases such as "failure is not an option," this actually denies ourselves the opportunity to move forward. In some fields of scientific exploration, experiments fail at a rate of 70 percent. With that level of failure, you would *have* to learn how to reframe failure just to go into work every day. Being able to determine what kind of failure happened assists you in reassessing how to move forward with your Great Work.

The first kind of failure is deviance. You opted out of following the process you selected for yourself. You didn't go to the gym, you didn't use glamour as a weapon, you didn't do the ritual work, you didn't send your résumé, you didn't exchange social media with a new contact, you didn't hit your word count, or you didn't show up. The only way to solve this kind of failure is to do the work you set out for yourself.

Inattention is the next cause for failure. You forgot to water the plants, you didn't follow up about your college application, you started magic that requires regular attention but got distracted and let it die like a bowl full of sea monkeys, you stopped putting care into your glamour and let it wither. The solution to this kind of failure is obvious: pay attention to the details of your glamour and your Great Work.

A lack of ability can sometimes cause failure because you don't have the skill set to complete the tasks you set out for yourself. You've never been on a date, you've never had a career, you've never had a child, you've never spoken French, you've never performed the rite you are working on, you've never tried to use glamour to get what you want. There's a learning curve involved here and the best resolution to this kind of failure is to keep practicing until there's improvement and to work on gaining the skill sets you need through further education.

Next, we have what's referred to as process inadequacy. You followed the syllabus, showed up to class, read the book, but still could not understand cell division; you followed the IKEA directions perfectly but your bed is more of a wood pile; you have worked with your glamour as suggested and still can't tell if it's working. In this case, you are reasonably competent but something about the explanation is not clicking. It could be because the instructions were not correct to begin with, but it could also be because it's not being explained to you in a way that is connecting with you. In these cases, see if someone else can make sense of the directions. If they can, ask them to explain it to you in another way. Step away from the issue for a little while, take a breath, and try to look at it a different way to see if you can work it out. If the instructions were never correct, do your best to find an alternative explanation such as watching someone put together your bed on YouTube or using different tools.

Process complexity explains when the task you are attempting to complete is too complicated to reliably complete every time. Think triple axels in figure skating, baking a soufflé, and glamour. There are so many factors involved with many out of your control. In this case, you need to accept failure as a critical component to executing more complicated tasks in your Great Work. Consider if there's anything you could improve or strengthen (here's a hint, in most cases the answer is *yes*) and assent to sometimes falling on your ass as part and parcel to doing these difficult undertakings.

Your inability to take every event that has happened in the past, present, and future into consideration could also lead to failure. You burned a bridge five years ago with a contact that would be critical to your current Great Work, you didn't notice that the weather today would be unfavorable to an outdoor event, and you didn't know that ten years from now your industry would crash. In this particular kind of failure, all you can do is stay on top of all potential events you can be aware of while looking at your constellation net and accept that you are not omnipotent (yet) but neither is anyone else.

Sometimes you may be testing a theory to see if it works. Will drinking more water make your skin glow? Will you be able to flirt at a friend's party? Will going to the gym three times a week give you more energy? Will presenting yourself at an important event as your most glamorous self grant you your heart's deepest desire? You are play testing these theories, which means that since they are unproven, there's always the chance that they may fail as they may need more fine-tuning for success. Maybe you can only bring yourself to talk to your friend at the party, so before his next party you will ask your friend to bring you into a discussion because you're shy. You need to tweak your hypothesis before simply giving up and account for variables that could have led to failed testing. Fine-tuning requires critical thinking skills both for your glamour and for your practical work.

Finally, there's exploratory testing, which is where you are experimenting to expand your knowledge base by looking into previously unexplored opportunities that lead to undesired results. You did everything you needed to do for the new job. You used your glamour skills, you did all the practical work and . . . you hate it there. There are a few ways you can deal with this: Structure your glamour and practical work loosely as discussed earlier so that you are willing to take some chances to go off-path and see where your goddesses and spirits lead you while accepting that what other people/deities/spirits think is good for you may not be what *you* think is good for you. You are not a slave; you are welcome to have a difference of opinion. We all want a Great Journey where we can clearly trace our path to success through our failures but the truth is sometimes mistakes are simply that, mistakes. You wanted to go in a direction, you went in it, and it didn't work. It doesn't always lead to epic victory—sometimes it was just a detour. The more you can accept that, the more you'll be able to think on your feet. Do you want to give the job some time to see if you can learn to like it while working to change the aspects you hate through glamour and practical work? Do you want to start a side business so you have a place to be creative while still getting a solid paycheck? Do you want to immediately start job hunting? All of these are options are valid, so you need to discover which will be best for you.

You Are the Common Denominator

The more accountability you can take for your part in a failed aspect of your Great Work, the more you will be able to think creatively and find a new strategy. Think about it this way, which scenario has problems that you can take action about more immediately:

1. You have a ramen stand in Tokyo, and with no notice at all, Godzilla comes through and crushes it.

2. You have a ramen stand in Tokyo and you hired your sister to run the cash register and she has a spotty work performance record, your noodles are a little undercooked, and you have not been using social media to promote your ramen stand.

Obviously, scenario one is natural disaster in this world. All you can really do is hope that your ramen stand's insurance policy covers acts of Godzilla. But how often in life is destruction and ruin completely out of your hands and solely due to outside forces? Rarely. In scenario two, you can blame your sister for showing up sporadically, you can blame your stovetop for its inability to cook your noodles to the standard required, and you can blame your Internet for its spotty WiFi, or you can accept responsibility for your part in this. *You* hired your sister. It is your job to ensure that she shows up when she's supposed to and if she doesn't, you need to fire her and hire someone more reliable. *You* chose the stovetop. You can figure out how to compensate for your noodles using it or buy a new one. *You* know how important social media is to your small business, so it's your job to find a better provider and to set aside time every day to give updates about your business that will help your brand be more visible.

It is incredibly unlikely in any failure that you have no accountability for it. Divorce, break-ups (with family, with friends, with relationships), finances, career issues, creative pursuits, all of that has something in common: you. That doesn't mean that there were no mitigating factors from outside influences and it doesn't mean that there weren't external forces at work. But the sooner you can figure out what you were truly responsible for, the sooner you can take action to make changes as needed.

Let's get personal. In my first marriage, my husband walked out on me and told me we were never, ever getting back together because I had personality problems. I had failed in my marriage. We were together for seven years prior to getting married, but there I was not even a full year later, an abandoned bride with a frozen uneaten tier of wedding cake that would never be shared together. He was done with me and our marriage, and no amount of tears or begging and pleading was going to change that.

I was so floored and shell-shocked, all I could eat was bleu cheese and sun-dried tomato-flavored Triscuits for weeks. I was completely emotionally ruined and didn't know if I was also going to be financially ruined, just to rub some salt and lemon juice into it. Here's the thing though: I couldn't control him or his actions. I couldn't make him be kind or cruel to me; I couldn't make him give me a reasonable settlement on the debt in my name that I foolishly agreed to rack up together (though he ultimately would settle with me eventually); I couldn't stop him from signing legal documents in a specific time frame. All I could do is figure out what I could do and try to focus on that instead of what he would or would not do.

I could (and did) consolidate my debt into a back-breaking payment I could make monthly for six years, I could figure out what I did wrong in that marriage so I could grow from it—not what *he* told me I did wrong, but what *I* told me I did wrong. Did I communicate excellently about relationship matters? No. Was I fiscally responsible? No. Was I often jealous and passive-aggressive? Yes. Did I like to wind him up? Yes. Did I prefer to be right instead of happy? *Always.*

I can work on all of that. Am I perfect now? Of course not, but I can accept these flaws and try to figure out how to be a better person (and partner) while accepting them. Reflecting on my flaws was a relief to me. It meant I wasn't looking for some external force that came in and wrecked everything. *I* helped wreck things. That means I can fix them, too. Owning my flaws means just that: I *own* them. They don't own me. I decide how to fix things. I decide how to work through them. I decide to take responsibility for them. It is so freeing!

When you are able to take responsibility for when parts of your battle plan for your Great Work fail, it opens you up to better reassess your situation. You can figure out where you missed opportunities, what parts of the plan need to be re-imagined, if you need to start over completely, if what you thought you wanted is actually what you wanted, new unexpected paths to explore, and what flat out didn't work for you.

When (not *if,* if you are doing this correctly) you fail, it is obviously very discouraging. No one likes to make mistakes, no one likes to be rejected, no one likes other people doing the "I told you so" dance. Plainly, it feels like shit. You were wrong, others were right, no one wants your art, your magic doesn't work, no one wants to date you, no one wants to have a baby with you, no one wants your skill set, no one wants to help you. That is flat-out depressing. Take a day or so to wallow in this mire. Really wallow. Teenager it up. Stare at the ceiling, watch *Melancholia* over and over again, cry, wear sweats, text your friends incessantly bemoaning your fate, and eat ice cream straight out of the container. After that day, it's time to pull yourself together and remember that you lost a battle, not the war. You'll know when you lost the war. Most of the time, by the time it happens you're relieved to no longer be fighting and you can figure out a new life for yourself in exile.

But today is not that day, most likely. Remember the steel in your spine, wipe the mud off your face, drink a smoothie, slap on some good clothes and do your hair up pretty, and figure out how you will win the next one.

Esoteric Experiment No. 15

Objective: Because failure can be so brutal and draining, it's important that you recharge your glamour.

Choose a location that is sacred to you: a wildflower sanctuary, your favorite park, your backyard, the field where your favorite Beltane celebration happened, your vanity, your altar space, under your dining room table. Be sure that it's a place where you can work. Wear your glamoured object and build a nest for yourself for your Work with wooly blankets, lacy shawls, soft pillows, and the books that you love best. Bring yourself into trance space and go to your internal sanctuary. You are going to call your glamour back to you. Think of each little piece as a glittering faery light that you take back into yourself in whatever method works best for you: swallowing, absorbing through your skin, merging with your spirit. What has taken pieces of your glamour from you? Your latest creative endeavor? All the work and Work that you put into your recent rejected proposal? Making your house glamorous for a date at home with your spouse? Actively engaging with your loved ones? Finding the right things to say, the right clothes to wear? Changing previous habits? That beautiful girl who slipped in extra flowers with your order? Call it all back to yourself. Your glamour is yours. You may choose to share it, you may have bits taken from you from those who want a (literal) piece of your shine, you may choose to expend it in the name of your Great Work, but it always belongs to you. Call your glamour back home to you. When you feel the return of your glamour in full, lick your finger and seal your glamour object with your saliva. Center. Soham. *I am that. I am the swan.*

In the
Valley
of Your
Hunger

Think on a time when you were sick with love and lust for someone. He didn't know that you existed, but all you could think about all the time was him. You tried to will him to just love you back or at least kiss you until your heel popped like a starlet in an old movie, but he never even spoke directly to you and probably never even knew your name.

Remember when you were in love with your best friend and she would hold your hand sometimes or brush the hair out of your eyes and smile at you like she wanted to kiss you forever and your heart would feel like it would become uncaged from your ribcage. You would stay up all night talking and get ready for the party together, and you knew everything about each other except that you were desperately in love with her. You had moments here and there where you thought maybe she knew, maybe she would *do* something about it, but you were too paralyzed to ruin everything. She never breathed a word that she knew how you felt until you drifted apart, and now you're not even social media friends.

Evoke the memory of when you were in love with your sister's boyfriend and how he smelled when you would hug each other, both holding on for just a few moments too long and how you would always fight with each other about the dumbest things so neither of you would have to face how you felt for each other, your sister unknowing that when she fell asleep on the couch you both would nearly set each other's heads on fire with the intensity of your unblinking staring into each other's eyes until she woke up. The one time he invited you over because your sister was at a band rehearsal and he wanted to show you a meteor shower with his telescope in his backyard and when you felt his breath on your ear, your knees went weak but you said you had to go home. They broke up a couple months later, he started dating someone else, and you never spoke of it.

Whatever iteration this forbidden attraction manifested in your life, think about how it made you feel. The way your pupils would dilate, your breath would catch, the acceleration of your heartbeat, the thrill that would pulse through your veins from the forbidden and unconsummated and what that felt like.

Austerity Is for Everyone

Austerity can do that for you. Austerity can take that anguish, that burning and yearning and make it into a blaze for your Great Work. It can make you hollow, beautiful, and glorious. On its surface, austerity may seem like something that is at a cross-purpose to glamour, but that's a very shallow reading of both austerity and glamour. Glamour is the tool you are using in your Great Work, and austerity is the whetstone you are honing your weapon against. Suffering for one's art has long been considered erotic, agonizing for one's lover, spirit, or goddess even more so. There's something about that combination of pain and ecstasy that has fascinated the average human long before *Secretary*.

Anchorites were the epitome of austerity in the early Middle Ages, and almost every village in England had one. As an anchorite, your only concerns would be to be engaged in prayer regularly, fasting and other devotions, offering makeshift confessions, eating the food that was given to you, and reading a lot. An anchorite would be given her last rites before entering her anchorhold as it would be expected that as she was sealed up into her anchorhold, she would first spiritually die and be spiritually reborn a living saint in her hold and then eventually bodily die in her anchorhold.

Her hold would be sealed up and she would be entombed in it. An anchorhold was attached to a church most of the time. It had to have three small windows: one facing out into the street where people would come and visit the anchoress and receive wisdom and guidance from her, an internal window facing the church altar, and a window for the anchorite's caregivers to tend to her bodily needs. Her hold would be about fifteen feet square unless it was part of a private estate. If you got to dictate the terms of the building of your hold, it was permitted by church law that it could hold up to two servants. Anchorite life was typically reserved for women (and men) of education as they were supposed to spend more time reading than in prayer.

It was a heady combination of being completely enmeshed in secular life and completely set apart by it. For a woman, this was an especially excellent opportunity as it meant that you would not be subjected to your husband's whims, or death in childbirth (though plague was still possible), and be allow to read and be left alone for most of your time while still engaging with the outside world. Anchorites were told to be careful not to put on airs, as they would have access to all the juicy local townie gossip as well as a special standing in the church, especially if they were female anchorites.

There was a rather liberal policy about male visitors and hands would creep through the window from the street for you to decide to dismiss immediately or clutch onto. You weren't even a nun, necessarily, and the only person you had to take orders from was your bishop who entombed you. Your confessor would oversee your decision-making process as an anchorite and keep you set on your path of various devotions and services, when you weren't literally digging your own grave with your hands for sport in your spare time. Depending on who you were betrothed to, this would still often be a more enjoyable life for many.

Despite (or perhaps because of) being walled in, it was a very freeing life for many anchorites. Your food would be taken care of for you, men were constantly trying to seduce you through the window, and you'd have a lot of time to write and mend clothing as well as command appearances from important people in your community when you weren't busy fasting, committing austerities, and receiving holy visions. This was an exciting amount of power for women especially to access. If you weren't leading revolutions as an abbess or plotting civil war as a courtly lady or queen, this was a good path to power and influence as a woman in the Middle Ages. It was however, a fairly limited path; even for upwardly mobile Middle Ages power girls there were only so many anchorholds to accommodate budding anchorites.

The Reluctant Wife and Prioress

While it is not known if Heloïse wanted to be an anchorite, it is certainly within the realm of possibility, given her desire to eschew marriage and family, stopping only for her passion for her lover. Heloïse knew what it was like to burn for her lover and lead an austere life. She fell in love with her tutor, Peter Abelard, when he moved into her uncle's home where she resided in France. Already the most famous female scholar in France, Heloïse was likely not too much younger than Peter and their mutual intellect inspired a flurry of passionate love letters between the two as they conducted a scorching illicit love affair under Heloïse's uncle's nose.

Birth control was not really on the table in the twelfth century, so all that love-making eventually resulted in Heloïse becoming pregnant. Peter sends Heloïse to his sister's home in Brittany where Heloïse gives birth and then likely foists off their child, Astrolabe, on Peter's family as her thoughts on children aren't especially enthusiastic when she wrote, *What man, bent on sacred or philosophical thoughts, could endure the crying of children . . . ? And what woman will be able to bear the constant filth and squalor of babies?*

When her uncle learns of their doings, he is furious. Getting knocked up as an unmarried young woman has started many hand-wringing reality television shows in the twenty-first century, you can imagine how well it was received in the twelfth century, especially since both parties were nobility and unmarried. Heloïse's uncle demands they get married, and Peter, feeling bad about the situation, agrees.

It is actually our budding twelfth-century radical (even by today's standards) feminist Heloïse who is completely disgusted at the prospect of marriage. She later writes to Peter, *I never sought anything in you except yourself... I looked for no marriage bond... if Augustus, emperor of the whole world, saw fit to honor me with marriage and conferred all the earth on me to possess forever, it would be dearer and more honorable to me to be called not his empress, but your whore.* Peter is very persuasive, however, and she is in love with him, so she reluctantly agrees.

Here is where things start to become interesting. Once everyone's on board, Peter essentially says, "Oh hey, this is totes a secret marriage. That's cool, right?" As we have learned from Elizabeth Woodville previously, that is completely uncool, Peter. In the Middle Ages, it meant you were up to some shady business. Heloïse responds with something like, "...Okay. I guess. As previously discussed, I, like, don't even want to marry you to begin with, so whatever." Peter comes back with, "Great! So, um, I'm just going to hide you away in an abbey until things with your uncle calm down." Heloïse is not particularly into this idea but wants them to eventually live like normal people and grudgingly consents. No one knows what Peter's intent was—it could have been to shield Heloïse, it could have been to make sure his reputation wasn't damaged (something he will personally set fire to himself a bit later), or it could have been he was feeling done with Heloïse and her uncle, trying to slither out the back door to parts unknown to continue being a philosopher.

We've already established that Heloïse's uncle has anger management issues. When he sees that Peter is potentially trying to dodge his husbandly duties, he gathers up a bunch of his bros and decides to attack Peter in his studio apartment. Heloïse's uncle castrates Peter, as one does in this situation, I suppose. Peter is now overcome with shame and remorse about his illicit affair, his crummy husbanding, his lovechild, and now has a physical reminder about why he was a bad pony.

He decides to take holy orders and decides Heloïse should do the same. Again, Heloïse is not very into this, but Peter has run off to a monastery anyway so what the hell, may as well become a prioress because she is still super brilliant. She likely figures they will see each other once in a while and will tongue kiss and continue their letters, a reasonable compromise for their situation.

For his part, Peter decides to not speak to her for twelve long years while he is busy nearly getting excommunicated for heresy (likely only saved from that due to his family's importance) and alienating every other monk he lives with until he's convinced that they are trying to poison him. He is a pain to live with and very self-righteous, so maybe. That said, he's still completely brilliant, and eventually Heloïse finds a document he wrote called *Historia Calamitatum,* wherein he has decided he forced himself on Heloïse and now feels super sorry about it. Heloïse writes him to remind him how passionate and awesome their love is, but Peter is having none of it, even when Heloïse (truly!) writes to him in detail about thinking about their sex life during Mass.

Completely annoyed, as she wanted neither to be married nor a nun but has only done both for Peter due to how crazy in love with him she is, Heloïse thinks to herself something along the line of:

"He doesn't want to get all *Thornbirds* with me, fine. But I'll be goddamned if he thinks he can ignore me. I have not put up with all of this nonsense at the abbey for twelve years doing everything that is boring and terrible for Peter to simply self-flagellate for the rest of our lives and be completely unbearable as a correspondent to add insult to my injury. I will politely tell him that he's a jerk and has caused me nothing but sorrow for the last twelve years while I've been doing nothing but thinking about him while living in this dump with these psychotic women, and tell him I will no longer speak of this to him. Instead, I will change the rules of engagement and remind him that I'm capable of speaking about all of this tedious God stuff, too. I will ask his opinion about every difficult detail of the Bible that I can think about so he pulls himself together and has some more impressive writing to show for it, at least. Meanwhile, I guess I'm stuck managing this nightmare so I guess I'll get good at it."

They exchange long, thoughtful letters about the mysteries of Christianity, and Peter writes some really great things inspired by Heloïse. As they both were aging, he wrote to her to ask to be buried beside her, which made enduring all of this garbage at least somewhat palatable to Heloïse, who now feels content to have served as his muse and secure in the knowledge that his life was completely meaningless without her and they died, happily ever after.

Lessons from Hel

You may still be dismissive of austerity as a Witch; understandably so. Heloïse sure wasn't into it by choice, though she learned to lean in. If you had decided to cast off the shackles of sin and run toward debauchery as you embraced Witchcraft, it sounds terrible. If you felt oppressed by other people in power telling you what to do as often they told you what *not* to do as well, nothing about austerity sounds appealing when you could be engaging in the more enjoyable worldly pursuits such as dancing naked around a bonfire; engaging in hot sexual affairs with whomever(s) you have chosen; and consuming a decadent amount of red meat, cheese, and chocolate while drinking and smoking everything that isn't nailed down. It's understandable that you are not eager to voluntarily give these things up. Most of us don't like being told what to do.

Freeform Austerity

However, here is where real austerity (instead of rote austerity you are performing to please others) gets sexy. No one is telling you what to do. *You* are telling you what to do. You are deciding what to set aside, for how long, and to what purpose. This is an excellent use of your time for many reasons: if you are constantly engaging in blood orgies or sloth or whatever your worldly pursuit of choice may be, you start to become jaded to it. The more cynical you become about your excesses, the less interesting they are to you as a person. You will hopefully lead a very long life, so having periods of voluntary abstention will assist you to not become tired of everything you once enjoyed. Too much in the world will also leave you satiated, slow, and lazy. Austerity will burn away that slowness, especially if you are willing to dig into those vices that give you the most trouble.

In Hinduism, a religion that pre-dates Christianity by about fifteen hundred years, austerity is called *tapas*. When you are performing tapas in Hinduism either by choosing to refrain from specific vices or performing specific difficult tasks such as sitting in front of a bonfire at noon in summer, sitting naked in the snow at night in the winter, standing on one foot for an extended amount of time, meditating for extended amounts of time, performing *japa* (mantra using prayer beads) for long periods of time, and other difficult tasks, you are raising heat to either burn off previous wrongdoings or to possibly end the universe if you are so inclined. This is why the Hindu goddesses do their best to distract you with material gain, so that you can't ask for favors that will cause nothing but problems but they will be honor bound to give you. Hindu lore is filled with examples where people and demons did extensive amounts of tapas and nearly broke the universe. It's also filled with stories of devotion and how tapas can bring you your passion, even if you want to marry a god.

Parvati Likes a Boy (God)

In her first incarnation, she was Sati. Sati was to marry Shiva, but Shiva runs with a really rough crowd of cremation ground dudes that look like they were part of a Guillermo del Toro movie. As you can imagine, this goes over about as well as you would expect it would with a very traditional father. Sati's dad is horrified and immediately begins to talk to anyone who would listen about how horribly behaved Shiva and his crew are. Sati is so ridiculously in love with Shiva and is so embarrassed by her father, she chooses to sets herself on fire.

Shiva goes completely crazy because he was desperately in love with Sati. He goes on a rampage, refusing to willingly part with her body and destroying everything in his wake. Eventually, Vishnu is able to take Sati's body for burial and talks Shiva down. Shiva doesn't want anything to do with the world anymore, so he goes into a catatonic meditative state.

Enter Parvati.

Parvati's parents wanted her to marry someone who wasn't in a coma with really poorly-kempt dreads. Like . . . anyone else. But Parvati was determined to marry Shiva and wouldn't hear of anything else. She starts performing *tapas* to get his attention. Her parents figure she'll grow out of it. But Parvati is *so* determined to marry Shiva that nothing can stop her. She launches into a full training/*tapas* montage, determined to get his attention through the heat of her intention. She stops eating meat, rice, and even leaves until all she eats is air. She sits nude in the snow and wears her winter clothes in the summer in front of a blazing bonfire. *Look at me. Look. At. Me.*

Years go by and her austerities become more and more intense until the heat she is generating, the strength of her devotion, and her beauty awaken him and he realizes she was Sati and now has come back as Parvati. He immediately rejoins the world and falls in love with her. They get married and spend an eternity together laughing, fighting, making up, making love, and keeping the world moving.

Lessons from Parvati

Austerity demonstrates to your goddesses, spirits, and people around you that you are serious about your intention with your Great Work; it's how Parvati managed to snag Shiva. It demands attention as it shows your dedication. It's why it's part of just about every world religion—Hinduism, Buddhism, Judaism, Christianity, and Islam. Much like our other weapons we've discussed that are less enjoyable than simply buying a new lip gloss and calling it a day, it is still a tool you have the ability to use and should not be tossed on the ground, dismissed out of hand. Giving up vices for specified periods of time creates space inside yourself so you can become hollow enough to make room for new concepts, dreams, and ideas to take root inside your inner terrarium.

Austerity Is Both Revelatory and Tedious

With enough devotion, ideas will become flora and fauna that you never knew existed inside yourself. You will find strength and energy you never knew you had. You will first feel the heady toddler rush of saying no to something you wanted to say yes to. You will feel the longing and burning for that thing you have chosen to forsake. You will be able to taste, see, touch, and smell it without actually imbibing in it. It will be a mystical time of grand revelations and endorphins when anything feels possible and nothing scares you anymore. But then you will be tired, angry, sad, and you will feel like your austerity is meaningless because the contact high has worn off. No one around you seems to understand what you are doing and why you are doing it, and you have begun to lose sight of it yourself. Your austerity has started to feel like endless toil and drudgery. You start looking for ways to cheat your intention. It's not really a second portion if it's different food that didn't fit on the plate. Drinking vodka is okay because you gave up wine. It's not sex if you are sceneing at an S & M club. What will it matter if you just cheat once? You *know* that you know better; you know that your goddesses and spirits will know better too. So you burn in misery, without any of the rush, sometimes quibbling over the specifics for relief. But you keep working at it.

Sound familiar? Like your Great Work, perhaps? Austerity is one of the hardest kinds of glamour you can perform: one part opera, one part performance art, and one part interpretive dance. It showcases how much you are Other, how much you've *chosen* to set yourself apart, it shows that you are in a staring contest with the universe and you're starting to feel lucky. It's tedious and difficult but when you aren't making traction in your Great Work, it can open doors that were previously closed to you and help you find secret passages you didn't know existed. It requires you to be brave, motivated, and true. It also requires some serious thinking because you should never, ever make a vow to your goddesses and spirits and then break it. Why? If you think you had problems before, well, a vow is a serious thing and they take them very seriously. Failure to hold up your side of the bargain will likely result in crossed conditions and even less progress in your Great Work. Don't overpromise, just deliver.

Esoteric Experiment No. 16

Objective: Undertake an austerity.

Dress for the black ops mission that you are about to undertake. Write your intended austerity in exact detail, including any exceptions and the length of time you are undertaking this for. Your missive should be sealed in red wax with something from your person that matters to you—a braid or a lock of hair, blood drawn from your finger, or a jeweled piercing. At midnight, go to a crossroad. Bring offerings of your austerities and your letter. Use your glamour to give an invocation to the universe, your goddesses, and spirits about what you will be giving up so that they will notice you. Give an impassioned cry for all that you desire. Leave your offerings and your desire at the crossroads, and don't look back. Embark on your austerity as you let the world burn inside you.

Glamour and Great Work Final Check-In

1. How will you work with others to achieve your Great Work?

2. How will you use your glamour to influence others?

3. How will you overcome hurdles to achieve your Great Work?

4. How will you use glamour to keep yourself inspired?

5. How will you use your glamour and practical work when you are in uncomfortable situations?

6. How will you manage failure in your Great Work? How will you manage success in your Great Work?

7. How will you make austerity part of your glamour?

8. If you have not achieved your Great Work yet, what do you need to work on to get there?

LEVELING
UP

I was doing the thing I swore I would never do. I was already covered in someone else's blood, there was graveyard dirt in my ballet flats, the taste of tears was in my mouth, and I was gingerly feeling around a dead goat, getting goat's hair all over me.

Hecate. You and your damned ring quest.

> And I, the mistress of your charms,
> The close contriver of all harms,
> Was never called to bear my part,
> Or show the glory of our art?
> —Hecate, *Macbeth*, Act 3, Scene 5—

Sometimes Initiatory
Experience Happens in a Warehouse

The closest to that Greek theater/initiatory experience that I've gotten in life is seeing *Sleep No More* in New York City. First, you're wearing masks and you're not to speak. Second, each room is amazingly detailed as it took more than four hundred volunteers to put the rooms together. Third, they separate you from whomever you came with so that you can have a solitary experience.

Mash up a silent, super sexy modern dance version of *Macbeth* with *Rebecca*, put it in a huge warehouse that you've turned into a world from the 1930s containing a hotel, infirmary, insane asylum, graveyards, and woods, and you've got the performance, more or less. Each performance lasts about an hour and then (mostly) loops three times to give you a dream-like experience. There are smells everywhere along with music and dramatic lighting. You're allowed to follow whatever characters you like and ransack the rooms at your leisure (they have stewards/guides watching you, masked and silent). If it gets to be too much, you can hang out at the bar which looks and sounds like a club in an old movie where they have actors and musicians singing and you can remove your mask. Sometimes, a celeb du jour will sneak in and sing "Summertime" at the club while the performance is going on.

All during the production, rooms are opening and closing (and locking and unlocking) so you're never sure where you've been or what you've seen. If that wasn't enough, there are rooms that only a few people will get to see a night because an actor has to take you to them. It's been estimated that anyone who goes only sees one-sixteenth of the show in a night.

That particular night, I saw Hecate and followed her back to her lair. She ate raw meat from a locked container and coughed up a ring from it as delicately as a cat coughing up a hair ball and gave it to her chosen ghost-girl (ghosts refer to the audience). Zhauna Franks was playing her that evening. She seemed to envision Hecate as Marilyn Monroe as she was off the set from a movie. She flirted, she played, but she had a razor's edge underneath her and an obvious intelligence about her, and it was one of the most glamorous things I had ever seen. When she was playful, it was so genuine and sincere which made her performance that much more nuanced because it also made her sharpness that much sharper.

She then took the stage in the abandoned club and proceeded to give her performance of "Is That All There Is?" As I watched Hecate morph from all of those life change moments, sometimes laughing, sometimes smiling sardonically, sometimes filled with joy, sometimes crying her heart out only to laugh again, something inside me just *broke*. Was this all there was? Would it ever feel like enough, no matter how much I succeeded? I started sobbing behind my mask, my hand unconsciously clutched at my crow skull necklace and the other circled around my stomach. It was too loud for anyone to hear me. I was masked, and it was too dark for anyone to see me. I turned my face from her and brushed the tears from under my mask as surreptitiously as I could. I felt wrung dry and I wanted to be a ghost in the sea of ghosts, following quietly behind so I could process everything.

Hecate immediately zeroed in on me as she sashayed to the other side of her den. She put her hand on my shoulder, as if to give me comfort for a moment, and I relaxed under her hand. As soon as she felt me relax she got very close in my face and laughed mockingly. My shoulders slumped. If I'm being completely honest, even though I can't say what Zhauna's personal intent was exactly, my exact thought was, "the goddesses can be such jerks sometimes." I also knew that she was looking to see what I would do. I straightened my shoulders resolutely and looked her dead in the face, my gaze steady and resolute. She grabbed my hand, led me to her secret parlor door, and told me to wait outside it—she had something for me.

I waited. Only a moment later, she came for me.

She drew me into her private rooms and immediately took off my mask. I was scared down to my toes because being unmasked in the McKittrick (where everything takes place) feels like taking off your clothes in the middle of a church, but I was also grinning like a lunatic. I wondered if my makeup was smeared from crying and from sweat. She got very close to me and touched my face where the tears had been. She then gently but hopefully pulled underneath my eyes, possibly hoping to collect more tears. When there were none, she opened my mouth and poured a vial of tears onto my tongue. I swallowed obediently.

She started telling me a faery tale about a ship at sea, an arrogant boy, and a lost ring. She spun me around and dragged me into a pitch-black room while I was off kilter. She told the story while my breaths came in gasps and my heart raced in terror and excitement, sometimes whispering in my ear, sometimes howling it from a few feet away. While she was built like a dancer (small, slight, delicate) and I am not, she threw me around this pitch-black room like a rag doll, letting my body thump against the walls. She put my hand to one of the walls, which felt like grass, explaining how this foolish, vain boy had lost her ring. I tried vainly to find it in the grass even though I logically knew from the fandom-verse it wasn't there. She spun me again and hissed in my ear, "Find me my ring." She put my mask back on me and pushed me out of her room. I stood there gasping for a moment while a steward (the black masked attendants who are there to make sure we don't step too out of line) watched covertly.

My shoulders slumped again. My exact thought was, "The ring quest?! Is she serious?! WHAT ARE YOU TRYING TO TELL ME, GODDESSES?"

The ring quest, in case you're not familiar, is the Holy Grail of quests in the McKittrick, and not in a good way. Is it possible to complete? Yes. Are you about as likely to complete it as you are to win the lottery or get struck by lightning? Yes. The ring is hidden somewhere in the McKittrick. They move it every night. The McKittrick is roughly the size of almost a full city block. The ring is the size of an actual ring for your hand. *Vaya con Dios, sport!*

Previously, I swore never to look for the ring. It seemed like a colossal waste of time to me when you could be eating purloined candy and frolicking with Witches. Also, from what I had gathered from the fandom-verse, if you *did* find the ring, you'd be given another even more impossible quest, which would make me flip a table. Thanks, but no thanks!

I caught my breath. I dully tried to consider what it could possibly mean to me on a Witchcraft level (the game within the game for me at *Sleep No More*), that I would be sent on a quest like this. Even if I *was* able to complete it, I knew I would only be sent on a much harder quest.

Later, when recounting my tale to Jow over Indian food, he remarked, "So your reward for completing really difficult work is to be given even *more* difficult work?" I closed my eyes and briefly considered dashing my brains against the glass encasing the restaurant's sweets case as that has indeed been my life experience, and it's just as frustrating as it sounds. But it's true. It *will* only get harder. It's what success breeds. The better you do, the harder you have to work in artistic pursuits. There are very few actual overnight successes, if any. And if you *are* successful, generally it's expected that your future work should be even *more* successful. No pressure.

It is, however, difficult to ignore a direct order barked at you by a symbolic goddess. While my brain was spinning too much to process all this in the moment, I knew I was meant to go on the expedition as it was presented to me. I started looking for the ring. I went to floors I would usually avoid: the hospital with its torn up padded cell, wet clothes, and the smell of iodine in the air; the dirt-filled cemetery with its creepy empty baby buggy; the maze in the woods with the taxidermied goat. I pushed myself to look places I would never look. Sticking my hands into dark fountains feeling their algae-ish bottoms, plunging my hands into salt cellars, unsure what was under the salt.

(**Side note:** I *hate* putting my hands into things. Like, I never liked finger painting as a child, making meatloaf is gross, and so on. I'll *do* those things when the occasion calls for it but I *hate* it and I'll go out of my way to avoid it.)

I was picking up everything I came across and shaking bottles and boxes, listening for a tiny *clink clink* so I knew if I needed to investigate further, opening drawers and teapots. The stewards watched me warily, but I was always very careful and very gentle, as well as mindful of putting everything back exactly as I found it. After a little while, they seemed to know what I was doing. Sometimes, I would actually catch them talking on their walkies as I was entering a room, though they would fall silent quickly. I didn't know if they were talking about me (likely not) but I wanted to shout, "Hotter or colder? I just need a hint!" I started to get to that trance/dreamlike place where I couldn't tell where I was going anymore or what floor I was on or where I had been. I was beyond worn out. I barely sat in the hours up to that point, but I was outside of myself by then, searching and searching.

I didn't find the ring that night, as you might expect. I drove back to New Jersey exhausted and worn thin.

Your Ring Cycle

Make no mistake about it: your Great Work is your ring quest. Hopefully, you will eventually find your ring. But it will not signal that your Great Work is finished; it is much more likely that it will mean that your Great Work is evolving along with your glamour into a more difficult journey with greater rewards and greater risks. In the musical *Into the Woods*, Cinderella starts her story by wishing to go to the festival; by the second act she's wishing to sponsor a festival. The song "Ever After" only lasts two minutes and twenty seconds. Two minutes and twenty seconds of contentment, satisfaction, and happiness out of seventy-six minutes of the entire musical.

The wishes get bigger, the stakes get higher, and every time the characters think they've finished, they need to go back into the woods. *You* are always, always, always going back into the woods. There will be moments of accomplishment and joy, but it is just that: moments. Savor them, be present for them, but accept that you aren't finished.

You are never finished with working/Working in this life until you drop dead, and then it's onto something new. It's okay to feel frustrated or even angry about feeling like you are just on to the next quest instead of having the satisfaction of having completed your quest forever and ever, amen. Once you achieve your current Great Work, take a victory lap. Celebrate however feels appropriate to it and be as present as you can be and be all in. Throw a party, have drinks at a fancy place with your significant other and bestie, eat a whole pizza, rove through your city consuming brunch until there's no more brunch to be had, buy fancy shoes, go dancing, go to a festival and make new camp friends, go hiking, do whatever feels most you and doesn't introduce new problems into your life.

After your victory lap (which should last a *week* at most) and when you are starting to feel adrift, seal the end of this Great Work.

Esoteric Experiment No. 17

Objective: End your current Great Work and
start the glimmer of your next Great Work.

Choose your favorite natural place: where the ocean is glorious, a tiny stream that runs through your yard. a swamp with cypress trees strewn with moss, a historical monument to a battle from long ago, a forest carpeted in wildflowers. Bring offerings that will be friendly to the land: fresh ground cherries, spring water, oat cakes, flowers. Bring a project that will free your mind, along with any provisions you may want or need to be comfortable: a delicate shawl you are knitting, a jacket you are embroidering, a letter featuring your calligraphy addressed to a friend, a good pen and a stack of cards that you like. Arrange your offerings in a way that you find pleasing. Offer it to any goddesses or spirits who have assisted you and thank them. Write notes to any humans who have helped you and mail them or give the notes to your humans. Take a deep breath and make yourself comfortable. Formally seal the end of this Great Work using whatever methods feel natural to you: write the intention down and then seal it closed and bury it or cast it out to sea, draw blood and use it to seal your Work shut, inscribe a beeswax candle with your Work and let it burn itself out. Let your goddesses and spirits know that you are sealing this Work closed by giving an invocation out loud that flows from you naturally. Settle into your

project until you find a natural trance space. What place appears
next on your internal palimpsest?

You started out with a small ask with your glamour. Something un-earned by you but freely given to you. Now your ask is much bigger—you accomplished your Great Work and you need to move on to the next Great Work in your ring cycle. You can do this by working through the Esoteric Experiments again in this book as they are meant to work cyclically. Work-ing through everything again will give you a chance to keep your glamour as a finely honed blade. To ensure that your glamour keeps shining and growing, you need to keep using it. How is your glamour different now than it was when you first started? What have you learned about using your glamour? What mistakes have you made? What trespasses have you made against your moral compass? Where has using your glamour been more difficult than you expected? Where has it flowed easier than you had anticipated? Have you been able to integrate your practical work with your glamour work so they flow together seamlessly? What has become easier for you, and what is now more difficult? You can ask yourself these questions at the end of each cycle and keep a journal of your answers so you can see where you've changed. Something that may have been easier in a previous cycle may be harder now and vice versa.

But now, oh now. Now, you've wiped out of your mouth the bitterness of being overlooked and overwhelmed. You've thrown off the cloak that was smothering you with rejection and societal expectation. You cast aside the shoes that scarred your feet with failure, idleness, and apathy. You've battled your way past your oppressors who said you would never make it to the throne room because you are Other. You've thrown down with your opposition until they were forced to cede their ground to you. You've drunk with the turncoats and convinced them to turn their coats again, by sheer force of your glamour. You are bruised, you are bloodied, you are exhausted. You're here. You're finally here. You own the space you stand in, flush with your glamour and the strength of your Witchcraft. The Moon card. The Star card. The World card.

What will you do?

Pick up that crown off the ground and never look back.

Acknowledgments

I would like to thank: Jow Scangarella, Fran Castellano, Melissa Castellano Cole, Elysia Gallo, Skip Drumm, Norma Hoffman, Ed Chapman, April Rucker, Brenna Barkley Stephenson, Bryan Lord, Faelan F. Malamor, John Minus, Allison Armstrong, Gordon White, Vicki Ply, Jared Norful, Bridgette Taylor, C, Nora Tempkin, Joshua Gadobois, Jason Miller, Christopher Bradford, and my Charmers.

Gratitude isn't a word big enough to circumnavigate my emotion.

Bibliography

Abbott, Karen. *American Rose: A Nation Laid Bare: The Life and Times of Gypsy Rose Lee*. New York: Random House, 2012.

Abelard and Heloise: The Letters and Other Writings. Translated by William Levitan. Indianapolis, IN: Hackett Publishing Company, 2007.

Anonymous. *Ancrene Wisse: Guide for Anchoresses*. New York: Penguin Classics, 1994.

Bialik, Hayyim Nahman. *The Book of Legends/Sefer Ha-Aggadah: Legends from the Talmud and Midrash*. New York: Schocken Books, 1992.

Castor, Helen. *Joan of Arc: A History*. New York: HarperCollins, 2015.

Clifton, Jacob. "Something About Survival." *Brilliant But Canceled*. December 17, 2012. www.brilliantbutcancelled.com/show/gossip -girl/new-york-i-love-you-xo-1xo/.

Coyle, T. Thorn. *Evolutionary Witchcraft*. New York: Tarcher/Penguin, 2005.

Doniger O'Flaherty, Wendy. *Siva: The Erotic Ascetic*. London: Oxford University Press, 1981.

Edmondson, Amy C. "Strategies for Learning from Failure." *Harvard Business Review,* April 2011.

Grey, Peter. *The Red Goddess.* Chippenham, UK: Scarlet Imprint, 2011.

Gundle, Stephen. *Glamour: A History.* London: Oxford University Press, 2009.

Hotchkiss, Sandy. *Why is it Always About You? The Seven Deadly Sins of Narcissism.* New York: Free Press, 2003.

Lahey, Jessica. "When Success Leads to Failure." *The Atlantic,* August 11, 2015.

Lee, Patricia-Ann. "Reflections of Power: Margaret of Anjou and the Dark Side of Queenship." *Renaissance Quarterly,* Summer, 1986, 183–217.

Machiavelli, Niccolo. *The Prince.* Mineola, NY: Dover Publications, 1992.

Meyer, G. J. *The Tudors: The Complete Story of England's Most Notorious Dynasty.* New York: Bantam, 2011.

Nehring, Cristina. "Heloise & Abelard: Love Hurts." *The New York Times,* February 13, 2005.

Taleb, Nassim Nicholas. *The Black Swan: The Impact of the Highly Improbable.* New York: Random House, 2010.

Tough, Paul. "What if the Secret to Success Is Failure?" *The New York Times,* September 14, 2011.

Index

MELANIE MARQUIS

the

witch's

bag of

tricks

PERSONALIZE YOUR MAGICK & KICKSTART YOUR CRAFT

The Witch's Bag of Tricks
Personalize Your Magick & Kickstart Your Craft
MELANIE MARQUIS

Increase your power, improve your spellcasting, and reclaim the spark of excitement you felt when you took those very first steps down your magickal path. The first book of its kind to offer solitary eclectics a solution to the problem of dull or ineffective magick, *The Witch's Bag of Tricks* will help practicing Witches boost creativity, improve abilities, and cast powerful spells that work. Whether your rituals have become rote or your spells just aren't working, you don't have to settle for magickal mediocrity!

Designed for the experienced eclectic practitioner, this guidebook offers advanced spellcasting techniques and practical hands-on exercises for personalized magickal development. You'll gain the skills and knowledge you need to custom-design your own spells and advance your mystical development. Breathe fresh life into your practice and take your magickal skills further than ever with *The Witch's Bag of Tricks*.

978-7387-2633-5, 264 pp., 6 x 9   **$16.95**

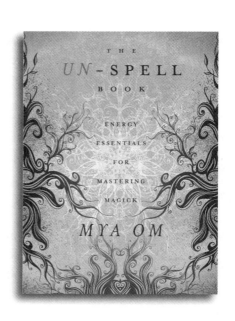

THE
UN-SPELL
BOOK

ENERGY
ESSENTIALS
FOR
MASTERING
MAGICK

MYA OM

The Un-Spell Book
Energy Essentials for Mastering Magick
Mya Om

Is quick magick as potent as long, complicated spells? Absolutely! You can create powerful magick anytime and anywhere, with few or no tools at all.

The Un-Spell Book begins with basic techniques that are necessary to prepare you for magick: grounding, focusing, setting the intent of the magick, and more. Then you'll learn new ways of raising magickal energy and harnessing it, discover how to do effective sympathetic magick, anchor your intent and energy to an object or even a word, and more. You'll also learn how to create thought constructs to carry out your magickal will.

No matter what path you follow, this amazing book will help you improve your magick and enable you to cast a spell for any purpose without having to rely on a traditional spell book. The power is already inside you, and this book will certainly teach you once and for all how to access and direct it effectively.

978-0-7387-2338-9, 192 pp., 5 x 7   **$14.95**

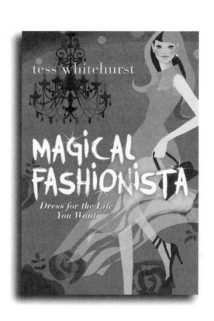

Magical Fashionista
Dress for the Life You Want
Tess Whitehurst

Discover how to use fashion to become your most gorgeous self, attract good fortune, and attract what you desire most.

Far from being superficial, fashion with intention can be a powerful, life-affirming practice. Popular author Tess Whitehurst explains how to build a wardrobe of beautiful items that enhance your attributes and personal magnetism. Discover how to select clothes, shoes, jewelry, and other accessories with simple guidance that will help you look and feel your best and manifest positive life changes. Put together empowering outfits every day—and for every occasion—with simple guidance on everything from the color, material, and pattern of clothes to gemstones, nail polish, and tattoos. Drawing on astrology, feng shui, the Wheel of the Year, moon phases, and more, this unique mystical fashion guide teaches you how to build a wardrobe of beautiful items that will express your true essense and attract what you desire most.

978-0-7387-3834-5, 264 pp., 5³/₁₆ x 8   **$15.99**